Who Gets to Name Grandma?

The Wisdom of Mothers and Grandmothers

2nd Edition

By *Granny-Guru*
Carol L. Covin

Published by 20 Minutes Press
http://www.newgrandmas.com

Copyright 2009, 1st Edition Twenty Minutes Press
ISBN: 978-0-9842862-0-1

Copyright 2013, 2nd Edition Twenty Minutes Press
ISBN: 978-0-9842862-3-2

All rights reserved, which includes the right to reproduce this book or any portion thereof in any form whatsoever except as provided by U.S. Copyright Law. For information, contact mail@newgrandmas.com

What Mothers and Grandmothers Are Saying

"Your wisdom is a wonderful bonus! I'm just trying to decide how I'm going to introduce my daughter and son-in-law to your articles."
Virginia Grandmother

"It's very balanced. May I send it to my parents?"
Mother of one

"I've got one for me and one for my daughter."
Louisiana grandmother

"As they say of Olympic gymnastics, you nailed it!"
Mother of an infant

"I received your book yesterday and thought I'd scan it during the commercials while I watched 'Dancing with the Stars,' which used to be a favorite TV program. Well, the TV program must not be as good as I remembered it because I couldn't tell you about any of it. I was totally absorbed in the book. It is clever, interesting and rich in thoughtful advice."
Grandmother of three

"Just read this. I think it hits the spot. It gave ME someone who understands me as well. So, I don't feel that I raised MY kids all wrong."
Two grandsons, one granddaughter

"I LOVED the article. It packed a lot of punch. I think it was very much on point and gave me some insight regarding my mother's thought process….I know she's not trying to undermine my authority – perhaps I knew that all along but this gently reminded me of that."
One son, one daughter

What Experts Are Saying

"This much-needed book should put life into perspective for both mothers and grandmothers, because it tells both sides of the story so well and gives such sensible advice."
Marguerite Kelly, *The Washington Post,* The Family Almanac advice column

"Congrats on a great book. I'm already looking forward to a copy!"
LeAnn Thieman, Co-author, with Jack Canfield and Mark Victor Hansen, *Chicken Soup for the Grandmother's Soul: Stories to Honor and Celebrate the Ageless Love of Grandmothers*

"A thoroughly honest, insightful guide for Grandma, or Nana, or Goddess, or whatever you choose to be called. Packed with good ideas for staying out of trouble."
Adair Lara, Author, *The Granny Diaries: An Insider's Guide for New Grandmothers*

"I LOVED it. What a great (and much needed) book."
Heather Allard, The Mogul Mom blog http://www.themogulmom.com

"A lively book that reflects many grandmothers' experiences. Easy reading and great fun! Despite the author's chosen title, one message is clear: no grandmother should set herself up as a guru."
Sheila Kitzinger, Author, *Becoming a Grandmother: A Life Transition*

"This is a fabulous addition to our library! I am sure guests will find it enjoyable and informative!"
Ben Powney, Activity Manager, Celebrity Century

"I finished reading your wonderful book! I loved every page, and found it very helpful. It should be required reading for every new mom and every new grandma. I'll recommend it to my support group right away."
Jenna D. Barry, author, *A Wife's Guide to In-Laws: How to Gain Your Husband's Loyalty Without Killing His Parents* (www.wifeguide.org)

Acknowledgements

Thank you, first, to all the mothers and grandmothers who let me interview them. I found them in all sorts of places. Mothers and grandmothers are everywhere!

- Family & friends
- Neighbors & classmates
- Church members
- Networking groups & trade shows

And, though any flaws in this book and web site are mine, I would like to thank the people who helped turn this concept into reality.

- Gabe Goldberg, Computers and Publishing, Inc., who has the sharp eye of an editor/writer, the generosity of a friend, and the largest network I've ever seen
- Paulo Sá Pereira, PRO-Marketing Graphics, a graphic designer who turns pictures into magic
- Barbara Keddy, Be Great! Marketing, who recognized my delight in becoming a Grandma and came up with my new name, Granny-Guru
- Gina Gaudio-Graves, of Directions University, for her strategic vision

And, especially, to my two perfect sons and my awesome daughters-in-law, who teach me regularly how to be great mothers today.

And, finally, to my two perfect grandchildren and the gift of their wonderfulness, which I will share with these two kidisms:
- "Grandma, you forgot to make your bed today." (dear Grandson, I did not forget. I don't have to be a role model anymore, and can be lazy)

- On being asked if her favorite word was "Why?" "No, 'Because' is my favorite word." (dear Granddaughter, I would add a close second is "Actually…")

Thank you forever.

Granny-Guru
Bristow, Virginia
April, 2013

Table of Contents

G – Interviews with Grandmothers
M – Interviews with Mothers

CHAPTER 1 11

NEWBORNS/BABIES 11

    WHO GETS TO NAME GRANDMA? (M) 12
    NOW YOU CHOOSE TO MOVE THREE TIME ZONES AWAY! (G) 16
    HELP THE MOM, NOT THE BABY (M) 19
    I MIGHT NOT KNOW WHAT I'M DOING, BUT I'M LEARNING (M) 21
    I AM NOT YOUR BABY-SITTER (G) 23
    HEY! THAT'S NOT YOUR BABY! (M) 26
    I AM THE PERFECT GRANDMOTHER (G) 28
    IT'S THE LAW FOR A REASON (M) 31

CHAPTER 2 34

TODDLERS 34

    THAT CHILD NEEDS A LIFE JACKET (G) 35
    DUELING GRANDMOTHERS (M) 38
    GUILT PRESENTS (M) 40
    BITE YOUR TONGUE (M) 43
    YOU'RE THE GRANDMOTHER, NOT THE MOTHER (M) 45
    IT'S GOING TO HURT THEM DOWN THE ROAD (G) 47
    I'D RATHER DO IT MYSELF (M) 50
    DON'T TOUCH MY DRESSER! (M) 52
    DON'T BE SO AFRAID (G) 54
    BECAUSE I'M THE MOM, THAT'S WHY (M) 57
    YOUR SON IS NOT PERFECT! (M) 60
    THE TV IS NOT A BABYSITTER (M) 63
    GRANDMOTHERS WHO DATE (M) 66

CHAPTER 3 68

ELEMENTARY SCHOOL 68

    DON'T YELL AT THE CHILDREN! (G) 69
    DON'T TREAT MY CHILDREN DIFFERENT (M) 71
    GRANDMA'S HOUSE. GRANDMA'S RULES. (G) 73

Why Do You Ignore Your Grandchildren? (M) 75
When Are You Going to Start Feeding Those Children Properly? (G) 77
Frisk Your Mother for Candy (M) 80
Back Off! (G) 83
ADHD Is An Explanation, Not An Excuse (G) 85
Ice Cream is Not a Meal! (M) 87
I'm Irrelevant (G) 90
Your Grandchild is More Important than Tennis (M) 93
The Money They Spend! (G) 95
I Would Like to Say Things Sometimes (G) 98
The Mouth On That Child! (G) 101
They Are So Ungrateful (G) 103

CHAPTER 4 106

HIGH SCHOOL AND BEYOND 106

I've Never Been Shy (G) 107
Give Your Child Some Relationship with God (G) 109
Tell Them You Love Them (G) 112
They Really Grow Up Fast (G) 115

ABOUT THE AUTHOR 118

Introduction

This book is an outgrowth of my first encounter with being a Grandmother, deciding what to call myself. As it turns out, lots of new Grandmas wrestle with this issue, thus the title of this book. Conversations with other grandmothers about this and other issues, and then, conversations with mothers to see if they had a different perspective (of course, they did!) were turned into the articles collected here, half based on conversations with Moms, half on conversations with Grandmothers.

The conversations usually started, "My Mom is great with our kids, but...." Or, "If only my daughter understood that...." And, across the in-law bridge, "I love my mother-in-law, but...." My daughter-in-law is a wonderful mother, but...." One of the first Moms I interviewed, for instance, led off with "Your Son is Not Perfect." She knew I had sons and, well, of course, they're perfect. This article, like all of them, takes a look at what each generation may be seeing in an attempt to understand the frustration that prompted the comments, and includes personal stories related to the themes.

Chapters are organized by the age of the children for which they are most relevant, from Newborns/Babies to High School and Beyond. This generally had to do with the ages of the children or grandchildren of the women I was interviewing, and the most pressing issues on their minds. But, it also helps to serve as a guidepost to those seeking to find others at their own life stage.

Enjoy reading the wisdom of other mothers and grandmothers. Enjoy the chance to deepen your own relationships. Enjoy thinking about your own precious children and grandchildren. Use these insights the next time you are sitting around the family table.

Relax, knowing your precious children or grandchildren are surrounded by love.

Thank you for sharing the journey!

Granny-Guru

Chapter 1
Newborns/Babies

Who Gets to Name Grandma? (M)

"I have a friend who is the second child in her family, but had the first grandchildren. She got very upset when her older sister later insisted on letting her child pick names for the grandparents and then demanded that my friend's children change."

New mother

So, who picks? The grandparents? The parents? The children? Is there really a right to the original birth order of the siblings, even if the birth order of the grandchildren is different?

I imagined that I was a very young-looking Grandmother when my children both announced they were expecting. Friends flattered me by agreeing. So, the question became if I look and feel too young for the old, wrinkled, stooped, gray-haired, rocking-chaired, knitting image we all assume goes with our culture and our own memories of our Grandmothers, then, what should I call myself?

One friend came up with the name "Glam-ma", short for Glamorous Grandmother. I loved it! When I announced to one of my sons that I had found just the right name for my new station, he and his wife were crushed, as I quickly saw by the shocked

> *Granny-Guru*'s **Grains of Wisdom: People's names are part of their identity.** Children can adjust to whatever the decision is – even if every child has their own name for Grandma.

looks on their faces. Her grandparents had all died before she was old enough to know them and her parents had both died within a year of their marriage. My son stammered, "You will be our child's only Grandmother. We thought you'd be honored." Well, of course, I am. And, that settled it. Grandma it is.

Who Gets to Name Grandma?

Grandma? Glam-ma?

I know of many families that wait until a child mangles the words Grandma and Grandpa and sets the pet name as Gamma, Gammy, Gam Gam, Paw Paw, Gamps or some such version that belongs to the first child who says it and the rest then learn it. It is an affectionate bond between grandparents and grandchildren. One woman told me the first grandchild in her family was dyslexic, so Grandma came out Mugga. The grandmother didn't really like it, but all the grandchildren that came after adopted it.

Others rely on cultural traditions for names: Nonnee or Nonna (Italian), Abuela (Spanish), Baba (Serbian), Bube (Yiddish), Lola (Phillipino). A young grandmother recently told me she is "Baba," because she was always singing "Ba-ba-ba…Ba-barbara Ann" when her grandchildren were visiting.

French-speaking Eleanor Roosevelt asked her grandchildren to call her Grandmère, also the title of a book about her, by her grandson, David. A recent survey suggests Nana is the most common choice, followed by Grandma and MeMaw.

In my own family, we used Grandma and Grandpa Last Name for two grandparents and Grandma First Name for the third. Grandma First Name, I found out as an adult, was my grandfather's second wife, some years after the death of his first. She never had any children and didn't like the idea of being called Grandma. She wanted us to call her by her first name. My mother thought this was disrespectful, so they compromised on Grandma First Name.

Some shorten this convention to Grandma First Letter of First Name, as in Grandma-O. A friend came up with G-Mom, which I think captures her impish spirit. A young woman recently told me her Grandmothers were "Rick-Rick" and Other Grandma. Rick-Rick being the closest she could come to pronouncing cigarette. The grandmother of 8-year-old twins told me she is "Grammy." A singer, she says, "This is probably the closest I'll get to a Grammy award."

Another mother told me that in her family the first grandchild was deaf, so signed Grandmother and the next grandchild continued the use of Grandmother. Later grandchildren followed the common Southern tradition of Memaw. Grandma still signs Christmas tags with the appropriate designation for each grandchild. Another Grandmother told me recently that she has a blended family, so natural and stepchildren's children have all come up with different names for her.

There are few other relationships where a name is so open to discussion and negotiation as that of what to call the grandparents. It is not a legal designation, but one of love. But, perhaps it is also one of power, as power shifts from one generation to another, or even within generations. Recognizing that power play may help shift the discussion back to love.

Children learn quickly that people have more than one name. Adults have one name for each other, another for their children to use, and another more formal name. Relationship names are part of a child's world from the very beginning. They will call their Grandmother whatever they are encouraged to – and, she will come whenever her precious grandchildren call.

For more stories and grandma names, check out our blog http://newgrandmas/names

Now You Choose to Move Three Time Zones Away! (G)

"Why did she have to pick this time to move?!"
Grandmother of a three-month-old

"OK. It was probably his job. Or, to be near his family. Or, maybe she really does not want me to be close by when she is raising my grandchild. I loved it when they lived near by, but, now, just when I have my first grandbaby, that's when they move?!"

Sometimes life is not fair. And, we have to adjust. Are you really afraid she doesn't want you to help raise that grandchild? Are you really too overpowering for her new mother instincts? It hurts not to have grandbabies close by. We must be hard-wired to want to help take care of them. And, there really is no substitute for their physical presence.

Plus, we have all this wisdom to share. And, we want to be part of their lives growing up. A second home. Another trusted adult. An extended family of love. My husband talks about how he used to eat lunch at his grandmother's home, walking distance from his own and from his school. Then, later, when she needed not to be left alone anymore, he often spent the night. An object lesson in taking responsibility for your family. Learned so easily and naturally as a child. How can we pass this on to grandchildren three time zones away?

I sympathize with this grandmother. I have one grandchild near and one grandchild far. We try to get the cousins together a couple of times a year. I treasure the unexpected treats of being asked to baby-sit overnight. But, we also keep each child one week in the summer when day care is closed. And, the far grandchild's mother, an avid photographer, keeps current photos posted on a web site for us to revel in as we follow our granddaughter's travels, her parties, her daily discoveries, her moods.

You can hardly talk to an infant on the telephone. So, what do distant grandparents do? Ask for pictures, sure. Videos can be emailed from phones right to your computer. Mothers these days are as likely to have a blog as not. Photo sites[1] like Flickr[2] or Shutterfly[3], where photos can be shared, are easy to use. Grandparents can be added to the invited visitors' list, so the photos won't be public. It's not what we're used to, but I wouldn't wait for a letter, hand-written by a Mom who's busy raising that beautiful grandchild.

> *Granny-Guru's* **Grains of Wisdom: Distant grandparenting requires more work and creative connections.** But, you are still their Grandma – an honored and cherished role. Define what that means in your family.

But, mail works the other direction, too. Postcards, notes and cards that Mom can read to your grandchild when they arrive, just to put you in their mind. I read of one grandmother who bought two sets of books, sent one to her granddaughter and kept one to read to her over the phone. Skype[4], a web-based long-distance phone service, can ease the cost of calling. Webcams[5] provide real-time video conferencing on your home computer. Apple's web camera is built in.[6]

---

[1] Description of photo sites: http://en.wikipedia.org/wiki/Photo_sharing. Review
[2] http://www.flickr.com
[3] http://www.shutterfly.com
[4] Description of Skype: http://en.wikipedia.org/wiki/Skype Skype site: http://www.skype.com
[5] Description of webcam: http://en.wikipedia.org/wiki/Webcam
[6] Apple with built-in webcam, iSight. http://store.apple.com/us/browse/home/shop_mac/family/macbook?mco=MTE3Mj A

I started a tradition of creating books around yearly themes like Hats! Feet! Balls! They include photos of everyone in the family. In the early years, they were ignored. But, I decided to make a copy for myself so I could read them to grandchildren when they visited. As it happens, distant cousins have reported this helps them feel connected too. The books also include old family photos, recycled instead of being relegated to a once-in-a-generation viewing when they are passed on.

$1 at Wal-Mart for 24 photo slots. You'll want to keep one in your purse.

Help the Mom, Not the Baby (M)

"Don't be a house guest. When you visit, don't expect her to cook for you. Let her parent your grandchild. You help the Mom."
 Mother of five-year-old, three-year-old and 9-month-old

This Mom has experience with help from grandmothers after the babies are born. All the grandparents are distant. Her own grandparents were already gone when she was growing up. She wants her children to have a good relationship with their grandparents.

She has read about other mothers on mothering forums choosing to wait three months before they allow grandparents to visit. But, she knows how much grandparents want to see that new baby and how hard it would be to wait. So, she tries to accommodate.

My own mother-in-law visited when our second son was a newborn. She vacuumed carpets and cleaned kitchen cabinets. And, I was really grateful. She did it without an attitude. She did not accuse me with sighs, looks, or comments about my not having vacuumed in awhile or not having cleaned out the cabinets. Rather, she took them on as tasks that would be helpful, not intrusive. She taught me that bay leaves set down on shelves keep roaches out. Who knew? I didn't think I had any, but it was nice to have clean cabinets smelling like bay leaves.

> *Granny-Guru's* **Grains of Wisdom**. Mom and baby are bonding, just as they should. Take this time to bond with the new Mom, in her new role. She'll remember and look forward to more visits.

But, mostly, she was there when I started to nurse. Anyone who nurses knows the first couple of weeks there is aching. But, a wet, warm washcloth works wonders. Since this was my first time nursing, such a common sense remedy, offered at just the right moment, was gratefully accepted.

There are so many ways to help. Showering attention on older children, who might be missing some of Mom's attention as she tends to the new baby. Laundry. Cooking. Especially treats for Mom and Dad. Freezing and labeling meals to be eaten when you're gone, if you know what they like. Cleaning. Errands. Picking up announcements. Addressing them. Mending? Do people still sew on buttons? Answering the door if neighbors visit. Walking the dog. I once thought getting a puppy when I was home with a new baby would be a good idea. Wiser heads prevailed.

Mom is sleeping, eating, nursing. There is not much time to dress, never mind entertain. A new mother once chastised me, "You didn't tell me I wouldn't have time to brush my teeth!" Cleaning waits for helpful hands or a baby that sleeps through the night.

And, what about the Dad? What treat would make his new life less stressful? Conversations about when he or his wife were children? Stories changing generational hands? Respectful, curious questions about how things have changed in the child-rearing world? That might inform later discussions about how you used to do it and why they're not doing it that way.

My mother-in-law understood this woman's advice without training. She pampered me. I pampered the baby. Happy visit.

I Might Not Know What I'm Doing, But I'm Learning (M)

"I am the Mother. They are my children."
Mother of three, two years apart

Boomer parents were likely to use their own and their friends' experience to gauge normal boundaries of behavior, and read lots of books. Today's parents will check the Internet to find out what's normal. Fast, efficient, reliable for many things, it puts child-rearing questions to rest quickly. And, they will read lots of books.

If they're still not sure, they're likely to pose a question to peers in an online forum. They don't have to wait for play dates or visits from Grandmothers. And, so much of what they need to know has changed since their mothers were in child-rearing mode. They're keenly aware of this fact. You have only to ask what vaccinations children get to appreciate the difference between when our children were raised and now.

Yet, sometimes, grandmothers and their perspective can be helpful. And, this young mother is not reluctant to ask questions when she needs advice. Think trouble pooping. Yes, this grandmother did have some advice to clear up the problem. The answer, by the way (BTW),

> *Granny-Guru's* **Grains of Wisdom. Boundaries need to be observed.** It's no longer your responsibility once you're the grandmother. Mix lots of love with the light salt of concern.

was blueberries. I would add to that, more fruit in general. Not dried fruit or fruit leather or fruit juice, but real, fresh fruit, a couple of times a day.

But, mothers are reluctant to start this line of questioning, fearing it will unleash an unwanted stream of advice that is not welcome, in exchange for the one piece of advice that is.

And, I must confess, it was friends, not grandparents, who convinced me to seek a diagnosis when my son was still not turning over by nine months. This is usually a four-month milestone. But, as he was normal in all other respects, and the doctor did not seem worried at six and eight-month checkups, I didn't worry about it. Finally, after several friends noticed and commented, I brought it up to my pediatrician at the nine-month checkup. He, still not worried, nevertheless made an appointment for a checkup at our local Children's Hospital, which specializes in unusual cases. Not wanting to wait for the appointment, I met with a local clinic that was available for free and they did a diagnosis the next day. "We don't know what it is. Probably never will. But, here are some exercises you can do that might help him get started." He started turning over the next day. I sent them charity donations for years after.

But, I kept the appointment at Children's Hospital several weeks later, just to make sure there weren't any related developmental problems. The doctor, wordless after her examination, excused herself to bring in a colleague, a new doctor in training. "I just wanted you to see what a perfectly healthy baby looks like," she told him.

Our perspective can be helpful, prompting a parent to get another opinion on something we think is out of normal bounds. But, it's also a good idea to let an issue drop once addressed. Save those observations for when you really need them.

I Am Not Your Baby-Sitter (G)

"I have a friend who was shocked when her mother said, 'Do not expect me to baby-sit. I already raised my children. I'm going to travel.'"
New mother

Just as with new marriages, new babies bring out expectations that you might not even know you had. Grandmothers baby-sit. Of course, they do. At every opportunity. You just have to ask. Right? Apparently not. This is a discussion, a negotiation, where unspoken expectations may not be accurate. So, you talk about it. Every time. The respectful attitude of parents should be: Would you mind baby-sitting at such and such a time, for such and so number of hours. Thank you very much. The attitude of the grandparents is likely to be: if that time slot is convenient, of course, we would be happy to. That's if everything is working and everyone feels they can draw limits when it is, indeed, an imposition.

But, sometimes that is not the grandparents' attitude. Sometimes, their attitude is, they're your responsibility. I've had my turn. Not everything turns out the way it is in the movies, does it? Grandparents as a back-up system. Grandparents anxious to spend time with their precious grandchildren. Grandparents who know how to offer enough advice, but not too much. Enough family time, but not too much. Enough gifts, but not too many. Some grandparents just won't play. Even if they could.

> *Granny-Guru*'s
> **Grains of Wisdom:**
> **Baby-sitting is a gift, not a right.** All you can do is offer the opportunity, not expect it.

I once volunteered to work with mothers with poor parenting skills. One I was paired with told me about asking her mother for

Who Gets to Name Grandma?

I am not your baby-sitter!

help with her newborn. Her Mom refused. Said it was her job now. She was an adult, after all, with her own baby. It helped explain why this mother was so clueless about how to take care of a baby that she continued to hold her child on her lap, into toddlerhood, just to keep him from crying. At nearly three, he could not say a word. Her second child, while an infant, was left at a hospital because she did not know how to stop it from crying.

Why was this grandmother so distant? Had she had her own children very young and decided she needed to make up for lost time in her own life? Had she been surprised by children, resentful? Did her daughter have a history of self-destructive behavior that had tested her mother's limits one too many times?

The sad end to this story was that the mother gave up both children eventually. She was simply unable to cope with normal infant behavior. She was not unloving, just unable. And, she had no family support to bail her out, to teach her what was normal, what was unusual.

But, most mothers are not so bereft. They can cope just fine with their children. They just prefer to include their extended family in their children's lives. For all the reasons we understand – richness, alternate views of life, link to past generations, unconditional love. If baby-sitting isn't an option, those links will have to be built other ways. When Grandma travels, ask her to send postcards to her grandchildren. To tell them stories of her travels. Follow her trips on a map at home. Collect stamps from her letters. Left over coins from overseas. There's more than one way to include her in your children's lives. Without guilt.

Don't take it personally if Grandma turns out to be the Baroness, not Maria, in your own family version of *The Sound of Music*. It is her decision, and her loss. And, yes it is your children's loss. But, as they do not know any different, you can still keep them informed as to what Grandma's up to, as though she were a more active part of their lives. And, maybe one day she will be.

Hey! That's Not Your Baby! (M)

"I want to be the first to go get my kid when she's crying."
Mother of an 8-month-old

"Yes, when she first came home from the neonatal intensive care unit (NICU), we wanted to make sure she was always picked up whenever she cried, by whoever was closest. But, those days are in the distant past now. I don't want to walk into my baby's room when she cries in the middle of the night to find my mother-in-law holding her. That's my job."

To be fair, this mother understood that an only grandchild, who lived 3,000 miles away, might entice a grandmother to want to pick her up, hold her and play with her when she woke up crying, even at 3 in the morning. In fact, she might have thought she was doing the parents a favor, giving them uninterrupted sleep, while she tended the baby. But, when it continued to happen, the new mother began to feel her territory was being encroached.

Grandparents who only see a grandchild occasionally might not be keeping up with new rules. One visit – everyone picks up the baby. Next visit, baby tended by parents first. Parents adjust rules as the circumstances

> *Granny-Guru's*
> **Grains of Wisdom:**
> **Recognize your anger.**
> Find some neutral way to address it before it surprises you with its fury and damages the relationships you hope to preserve.

change and may not remember that these rules were different six months ago because their lives are intensely filled with a baby's schedule and needs right now. It is why parents do not understand what grandparents live with intimately. In the long run, in the measure of a child's life, time flies by. Well, at 3 in the morning it doesn't really feel like it's flying by. You just know that baby needs attention.

We recently kept our grandson for a week and his mother marveled at how much more he was talking than just a week before. That is our constant experience with grandchildren because our visits are not daily. My husband tells the story that his father told him of how he used to marvel over the changes in my husband as a baby. Every day when he came home from work the baby was doing something new. Magnify that by weeks or months of absence.

In this case, the mother did something smart before her anger boiled over into an unexpected confrontation with her mother-in-law. She asked her husband to talk to his mother privately. "Mom," he said, "if the baby wakes up in the middle of the night, we'll take care of it." And Grandma never did it again.

Young women have told me this split of responsibilities for communicating with respective Moms reduces stress on a relationship. While mothers-in-law might wish for closer communications, 25 years with a parent gives each shortcuts and assumptions that are simply not available to a new relationship.

I Am the Perfect Grandmother (G)

"I am the perfect grandmother. I don't say anything to my daughter about how to raise her children."
Grandmother of five

Is this really what we require for grandmothers to be perfect? Don't give me any advice, Mom or Mom-in-law because I will think you are criticizing me and I cannot take it.

There is no question that, in the beginning, grandmothers have unequal power. After all, they have been successful mothers. They have raised their sons or daughters to adulthood, marriage and parenthood. There are other measures of success, but this is the basic one. And, new mothers, in the beginning, are typically very uneasy in their new role of total responsibility for someone else's life. If they did not already know it, they are soon to be told on all fronts – if anything goes wrong, it is your fault.

So, what happens? First, there is the fear, real or imagined, that your mother or mother-in-law, invested with those years of successful parenting, will try to take over. Her opinions carry more weight than

> *Granny-Guru*'s **Grains of Wisdom: Grandmothers may be right, but you'll never know unless you let them offer you advice**. It is up to the new mother to set the bounds she is comfortable with, but it will be a test between the two of them as they figure out when advice is needed or welcome and when it is too much.

your instincts because of her experience. And, in the beginning, all you have are instincts. And, books you've read. And, the baby-sitting you did in high school. And, if you're not the first in your crowd, watching other new mothers with their babies, thinking what you would do in that situation.

The nagging feeling that your mother or mother-in-law is suggesting discipline that is too easy or harsh, feeding habits that are not healthy, or sleep routines that do not fit with your own schedule just does not stand up to her certainty.

A new mother, in addition to learning by feel what her new infant needs, has to learn by feel what is the right amount of advice to take from her mother or mother-in-law. It is a loss if she shuts this conversation down. There are going to be times when grandmother is right. If she cannot step in at these times, the new mother has to learn everything for herself. This generational loss of wisdom is not necessary to keep a healthy relationship. The key is to be open and receptive to advice, while not taking all of it to heart. Pick out what works and be thankful for all of it. This is not unlike reading lots of books and deciding which experts you agree with, in any field. It is just that becoming a new mother is so filled with emotion and guilt and fear that this lesson gets lost. And, sometimes, Grandma persists when she thinks you aren't listening or following her advice and gets her feelings hurt. You can't hurt a book's feelings if you ignore it.

Probably the most important story my mother-in-law told me about child-raising was the sad result of a father-son bond never restored after a friend of hers treated her toddler son as the "man of the family" for the several years his father was away for World War II. The son resented his father when he returned and never got over it. Taking this lesson to heart, I showed my own toddler son pictures of his father often. We recorded tapes for him and I showed our son the letters I wrote every day of the year his father was in Vietnam. The morning after my husband returned, our son shouted out delightedly, "Mommy, Daddy, a butterfly" and we knew our son's heart had kept a place for his father.

A grandmother may feel like she is being a good grandmother if she, understanding that her advice has undue weight, just steps back and says nothing. She does not want to be that mother or mother-in-law who is seen as interfering in a new mother's tentative steps in learning what it means to take care of a new life. She may understand very well that advice and suggestions will be heard as criticism. But, this goes too far.

A daughter or daughter-in-law could do worse than asking for stories about what she or her husband were like as babies. That's if their mother or mother-in-law hasn't already offered, a common reaction when we see our precious grandchildren and remember the time our children were that age.

It's the Law for a Reason (M)

"I have wonderful parents who take an active interest in their grandchildren. But, they only use car seats sometimes. It is deeply upsetting to me. If my parents can't be bothered to take my son's safety as seriously as I do, then I just won't be able to allow them to see him in an unsupervised way."
Mother who lost a baby at birth

When this mother was in a grief support group, she met a woman whose six-month-old had been killed in an automobile accident with the grandmother as driver. The infant was not in a car seat.

While state laws differ as to how long a child must still be in a car seat, from three in Iowa to eight in Wyoming, and whether taxis and rental cars are included, this mother's fear goes to the heart of every parent's responsibility for their children's safety.[7],[8] A grandparent's casual attitude about this is not only not in keeping with current state laws, it is disrespectful of the parent's genuine and well-founded concern.

This mother recognizes that when she and her brothers and sisters were growing up, there were no car seats. For that matter, when I was growing up, seat belts were new. There were public service announcements talking about how much more likely you are to be in an accident within 25 miles of home, so, just running out to the grocery store was no excuse not to wear your seat belt. I didn't have to listen to announcements for this message to work, though. One of my neighbors, a doctor's wife, drove to the grocery store when I was about ten. The parking lot there had a 25-foot drop-off below one edge. When she accidentally drove

---

[7] Discussion from a pediatrician, Author, *The Everything Father's First Year Book*
http://pediatrics.about.com/od/weeklyquestion/a/seat_laws_ask.htm
http://www.amazon.com/dp/B001C4AHW/?tag=carcov-20
[8] State by state requirements for car seats
http://www.elitecarseats.com/custserv/custserv.jsp?pageName=car_seat_laws

over the curb at the edge, her car hung by its back tires over the drop-off. The paper dutifully reported that she had been wearing a seat belt. We all knew that had she not, she'd have gone right through the windshield. No public service announcement could top that lesson.

Let's assume grandparents aren't purposely putting their precious grandchildren in danger. So, what's going on here? Grandparents who have safely raised their own children may feel, in fact, that their methods are fine.

> *Granny-Guru's* **Grains of Wisdom:** If you don't know and don't act, that's understandable. But, if you know and don't act, there is no excuse. If you're asked and refuse to follow safety guidelines others have discovered, you may lose grandparenting privileges.

I once knew a pregnant neighbor who continued to smoke. When asked, she replied, "Well, my first child was just fine and I smoked the whole time I was pregnant with him." These are people who do not understand the power of odds. And, which side of those odds you want to be on.

And, my goodness, it seems every time you turn around there is a new restriction. Car seats facing backwards for one age, forward a few months later, graduating incrementally with each few pounds or inches a child gains. Eventually, only in the back seat. How are you supposed to entertain toddlers when they are in the back seat? Checking car seats on airplanes. Transferring them when grandparents pick up from day care. And, the belts are so tight. Across the chest, between the legs. You would think they were pilots strapped in to eject from a plane. They can't be comfortable sitting for long periods of time in one position. Besides, it's hard to undo all those fasteners. You have to pinch hard at just the right angle. And, time-consuming. Especially if you have a fussy child who needs to get home for a nap. And, it's not part of a grandparent's daily routine, as it comes to be for parents. So, the changing details of the regimen can be hard to keep up with. Is it really that important?

Parents, informed by studies prompted by firefighters' deep sadness on encountering unrestrained children in the aftermath of a car accident, have found that it is that important. How could they do anything less? There are times when a grandparent may undermine a parent in the name of showing children a different way to be in the world. But, safety isn't one of those times. BTW, sitting safely in one position won't hurt a child. You can sing from the front seat, and point out the cows. Some things are non-negotiable.

Chapter 2
Toddlers

That Child Needs a Life Jacket (G)

"A three-year-old walking around on a pier without a life jacket. Muddy water. What if she falls in and knocks her head. I don't want to go to her funeral."
Grandmother of nine

Perhaps we loosen the bounds as more children arrive. Perhaps we think someone else is watching. Perhaps we think a child used to the water is safe around it.

Or, perhaps we get more cautious after years of reading about accidents around water. He was just here a minute ago. And, there they are. Face down. Afterwards, it is too late to be sorry.

At about eighteen months, children start to be aware of edges. Start to be more careful not to step off. But, it still takes a few years for this to sink in. And, jumping-off games still tempt children to jump where there is sometimes someone to catch. Such as the game with someone in the water and someone still on the pier. Similarly, running away is a toddler's game. Endlessly delightful. Until it's not.

My own son started playing this game at the age of three as he ran toward the edge of a concrete lock, easily 25 feet deep. There was no water in it. There was no fence around it. He had been in our circle at the picnic moments before, but got beyond reach and turned my call to return into a chase game, played many times before. A nearby adult gauged the

> *Granny-Guru's* **Grains of Wisdom: This is a good role for grandparents.** Their fears are informed by years of reading about accidents. Their caution may be reasonable. Their opinions come from broader experience and can provide a necessary balance.

That child needs a life jacket!

distance and the path our son was on. Realizing our son would not stop and we could not get to him, this friendly savior ran to intercept, scooped him up and returned him giggling. There were no words. We could barely cope with our horror and thankfulness the rest of the afternoon. Our son was never out of reach again that day.

This balance of independence and care can be hard to strike. I watched a *Dr. Phil* show a few years ago where a frantic mother had asked Dr. Phil to help explain to her husband that it was not appropriate to leave a loaded gun around a four-year-old, or to encourage them to jump off the garage roof. The father saw a path toward instilling fearlessness. The mother saw imminent disaster. Dr. Phil showed the father videos of what four-year-olds do when they are left alone in a room with an unloaded gun and told not to touch it. They last about two minutes before they are playing with it. Similarly, if taught they can jump off a roof when an adult is there to catch them, they will try to do it when no one is there. The father got the message.

Drowning is the second leading cause of accidental death among children from 1 to 14, according to Alan Korn, the Executive Director of Safe Kids USA.[9] Recent data compiled by the Consumer Product Safety Commission shows that almost 300 children under the age of 5 die a year in pools or spas.[10]

We know it only takes a moment. We are constantly gauging that balance between safety and freedom. Between judgment and independence. Between the care of keeping close and the danger of letting go. And, the bar moves every day. Every day a child is more ready to handle independence. More responsive to words, to commands, when physically out of reach.

But, some changes may come too soon. Let other opinions help inform your decisions about when to let go. And, when to hold close.

---

[9] http://www.safekids.org
[10] http://www.cpsc.gov/CPSCPUB/PREREL/prhtml09/09229.html

Dueling Grandmothers (M)

"We went to the beach with my Mother because she has a small place and we can't all stay there. Now my Mother-in-law wants to go to the beach, even though we often stay at her house, just so she can 'see the two children having so much fun'."
Mother of a toddler and an infant

This mother is spending so much time trying to be fair to both sets of grandparents that she welcomed a recent move out of town. And, she has learned what every parent of more than one child learns the hard way. There's no pleasing everyone. You can try to be fair. You can try to make sure each side has equal time. You can try to adjust to each one's circumstances or personality. But, they will always see what the other one has and want it.

Grow up Grandmas. This is not a contest. Put yourself in her shoes. You're just trying to shower your grandchildren with attention. What could be wrong with wanting to spend more time with your grandchildren? To capture mental images of their laughs, their giggles, their funny remarks. To store away to share with friends, to hold for those times when they are absent, to treasure when they are grown. You, unlike the mothers of your grandchildren, know all too well how fast time flies. And, now, without the demands of climbing the career ladder you once had, putting a roof over your head, raising your own precious children, you have lots of time to shower on those grandchildren.

> *Granny-Guru's* **Grains of Wisdom: Don't fret that the other grandparents are getting special treatment.** Be glad that your grandchildren are.

We've forgotten who's in charge here. The Mom. She's in charge because she has the responsibility. She's in charge because, at the end of the day, she's the one everyone will turn to to break the tie. She has to decide. Let her. You had your turn. You are not helping by making her choose between you. You are not helping by expecting the same thing the other grandparents have. You could help her by having a discussion about what she would like. She knows you love her children. But, what does she want from their grandparents? More attention? Less? Time alone with her family instead of with grandparents? How can she even have this discussion without hurting your feelings? How can you without acting like she's not treating you fairly.

How do you handle this with children? You set up a family culture of fairness. Reinforced by communication and action. Yes, you have to take a bath. Everyone takes a bath. Yes. You have to brush your teeth. Everyone brushes their teeth. We'll try to be fair in making sure our children get time with both sets of grandparents. With differences explained. I know you want to go with your brother, but he's older than you. You can go there when you are his age. The beach was a fun vacation, but we went there with my Mom because her house is too small for us to stay over there. Offer alternatives. You can't go with your brother, but you can go here. We're not going to the beach again, but we can do something fun in town.

This should reduce hurt feelings to those times when you don't abide by your own rules. I still remember, when I was seven, my mother insisted that I finish the tapioca she'd served for dessert. Our family rule was you have to taste new foods. If you don't like them, you don't have to finish them. For some reason, she decided to break the rule that night. I sat there, tapioca in front of me, until everyone else had left the table. And, I threw it away. After which, it was never mentioned again. I still hate tapioca.

I sympathize with these grandmothers. I want the same thing. But, it's petty. It's another thing the Mom has to balance. She's raising her children. Don't make her raise their Grandmothers.

Guilt Presents (M)

"For my son's first birthday, his grandparents brought a trash bag full of wrapped presents. Most of them are in the attic."
Mother of two under three

"I know my in-laws only get to see their grandchildren two or three times a year. I think they feel guilty about that, so they buy them lots of presents, including a really precious ride-on toy. But, we live on a busy street and have a small place, so, we've asked everyone not to give us big toys. They just end up in the attic, with all the other things there is no room for. The other set of grandparents abides by our rules – no big toys. They just give us a check and say, 'Buy whatever you want, and put the rest in savings.' They also live near by, and are willing to do what I ask."

Guilt presents. I ran into this phenomenon when I was in junior high. There was a doctor's family on our street. He worked all the time. But, they got more presents at Christmas than anyone else on the block. We all felt sorry for them, because we thought their parents were trying to buy them, to make up for the fact that they didn't spend any time with them. But, he couldn't change his hours and these grandparents can't change where they live. So, they try to connect a different way.

> *Granny-Guru*'s **Grains of Wisdom: It's not the money; it's the thought that counts**. Split some of that generosity into different, longer-term treats. That's how I got to spend the summer in Europe when I was in college. Thanks, Grandma. And, cash in the savings bonds to start my first company. Thanks, Grandpa.

As for size, just try to convince family to buy small presents. We used to drive twelve hours to visit for Christmas, in a Toyota Celica hatchback. Presents to give away to extended family of more than 50. And, presents received. Packed into a hatchback for the return trip. My husband. The packing genius. Started every trip in each direction by putting everything out on the driveway and finding some way to put it all in the car. With much gnashing of teeth. Two-thirds of the presents were stashed in closets, to be retrieved months apart, throughout the year.

Why not money? Family generally doesn't like to give money. They like to give gifts. Because children do not get warm, fuzzy feelings from money. And, if parents buy them something, children don't get the personal connection of a gift selected for them by a relative. And, what a relative is really looking for is a personal connection to the child. Especially, a grandparent who only sees the child occasionally. A grandparent who now has the means to buy much more than they might have given their own children at that age. Gifts are not only a substitute for time and presence; they are a connection to that precious time when your own children were young.

So, what is the answer? Boundaries and substitutes. Today's toys for children are just as cute as they can be. It's easy to buy lots of them. You think you are helping the parents out, so they won't have to buy them all themselves. But, children don't need everything that is cute. And, this is a tradition you can't maintain as children get older and gifts get more expensive.

A boatload of gifts is not appreciated by a child and not welcomed by the parents. A special gift, selected with care, for birthdays and Christmas should be plenty. I don't even take gifts when I visit because I do not want to set up that dynamic, "Did you bring me anything?" Yes, I brought you a grandmother.

Extra attention should be lavished on college or savings accounts. Not so warm and fuzzy as gifts. But, a tradition started when a child is young that can be the beginning of a conversation about responsible choices for an older child, one who might have a job and start to appreciate what Grandma and Grandpa have been doing for them all these years. Because, by then, the conversation is, we all know how hard it is to save for college, but, fortunately, someone loved you enough to add to the money you are setting aside from your job.

Bite Your Tongue (M)

"When my Mom and I disagree, we understand each other from almost 40 years of arguing. But, my mother-in-law and I don't have that history. She keeps offering suggestions that I don't follow and she doesn't realize that I've heard her, but, for whatever reasons, decided not to do it that way."
Mother of three under five

"I have a great relationship with my mother-in-law. She is a wonderful grandmother and is a professional in the childcare field, so she's pretty current. But, we disagree on a lot of child-rearing questions. And, she doesn't pick up on the fact that I don't need to hear it again."

How long to nurse? How soon to introduce solid foods? Isn't he sleeping too long? Eventually, this Mom came to realize that her husband and all his brothers and sisters had followed the same sleep pattern when they were growing up. But, her son did not. After research, they found that he was within the normal range of sleep patterns, if on the high end. Her husband informed his Mom. "He's normal, just on the high end." OK.

This is a common pattern in successful communication strategies across generations. Mom deals with her own Mom. Dad deals with his Mom. In this case, they took it a

> *Granny-Guru*'s **Grains of Wisdom:** Parents get to take the lead. They need to acknowledge suggestions, but grandparents need to watch for signs to step back.

little further. They agreed that Dad could not tell when his Mom was pushing her suggestions a little too far. After all, he was used to it. Instead, he'd watch his wife, and if she started to tense up, he'd intervene. "Mom, thanks for your suggestion. We'll look into it. Mom, we've considered the options, but we're comfortable doing it this way. So, Mom, what's been happening at home lately?"

I remember when I first brought our son home to visit the in-laws. We'd been stationed at an Army base when he was born, so he was three months old before anyone in the family got to see him, except for his aunt, who had made the trek out to visit when he was only a few weeks old. But, my husband and I had eloped only a year before, days before he was inducted into the Army, and half of our relationship before then had been long distance, so I had met very few members of his close, extended family. They didn't know what to say to me, but they all knew how to coo and ooh and aah over a brand-new baby.

After three days I broke down in tears and put my foot down. My husband conveyed my new rule. Anyone visiting had to talk to me first. Then they could hold the baby. Word went out and I got to know my wonderful new extended family.

My husband had his own strategy for dealing with his mother-in-law. I was used to being manipulated. He didn't like it. He'd take our children out Christmas shopping for a special bonding day with Dad when we visited and he thought things were getting tense.

When grandparents have a deaf ear, believe that their opinions are more important than those of the parents of their grandchildren, communication breaks down. After all, it doesn't feel like a discussion among peers. It feels like a lecture. They're our children. We don't need lectures.

Negotiating the boundaries of opinions versus information is tricky. Some things have changed. Some things are because of different parenting styles. Some things are in response to different children. It is that effort to keep communication open and respectful that is tricky but important.

You're the Grandmother, Not the Mother (M)

"My Mom jumped into our daughter's game with, 'Don't talk to your father like that. Go apologize to your mother'. It's not her place. She's supposed to be the grandmother, not the mother."

Mother of two

"OK. Our daughter was getting bored and starting to act out. But, we had it under control. It's not my Mom's place to jump in. She's the grandmother, not the mother."

We have this image of grandmothers. Older, kindly. Giving out treats behind Mom's back. Lax discipline because they like to sneak about subverting Mom and Dad's rules on those occasions when they get to watch the grandchildren. Because that's what grandparents do. Right? They show children there is another way to be in the world besides the strict way their parents are raising them. And, it's ok. Everyone wants to go stay with Grandma and Grandpa because it's fun. You get to do things there you don't get to do at home. We know children can tell the difference. And adjust.

> *Granny-Guru*'s **Grains of Wisdom: You're not going to agree with everything the mother of your grandchildren does.** But, leave her the space to make decisions that don't involve safety or long-term harm. Sit back. Enjoy your beautiful grandchildren. Chill.

Except when it's not. We understand the Jane Fonda model of a grandmother in the movie *Georgia Rule*[11],[12]. Mom's life is a little out of control. Teenage daughter, Lindsay Lohan, is sent to live with Grandma for the summer before starting college for one

---

[11] Movie review http://movies.nytimes.com/2007/05/11/movies/11geor.html
[12] Get the movie, *Georgia Rule*, from amazon here: http://newgrandmas.com/georgiarule

last try at teaching her some self-discipline. Grandma eats oatmeal and blueberries for breakfast, a sign of old-fashioned values, gets granddaughter a job in an effort to instill responsibility, and doesn't take any nonsense from her.

But, what if Mom's life is under control? What if her children are well-mannered, polite? What if she is right there when her Mom decides to take over? When does support become interference? Couples learn early that their children will divide and conquer if they don't present a united front. So, they learn to back each other up. "Your Mom said no. It's no." "Your Dad does not want you to do that. Stop doing it."

And, single Moms, perhaps, can use the support of a sympathetic relative to provide similar support. "Don't talk to your Mom like that," from a close relative, reinforces the fact that adults agree. Children must treat adults respectfully. It's a lesson we reinforce because we know there are going to be many situations in a child's life later on where respect for authority is important. Church. School. Job. Police. Courts.

How to balance these two roles? Teaching a child respect for the authority of their parents. Letting parents set the bounds of discipline with their children. Because stepping in, while the parents are there, sends the message that you don't think they are doing their job. Is this what you really believe, or are you naturally falling back into your former role as teacher or parent, when you had to set the rules.

I vote for when the parents are there, they get to set the boundaries, unless you think your grandchildren are in danger or wildly out of control. They are teaching you what they think the rules should be. There will be a test. If you pass, you get to keep the grandchildren at your house. The rules can be different there. The grandchildren will adjust.

It's Going to Hurt Them Down the Road (G)

"They laugh when their sons misbehave. They think it's adorable. When their son stomps his feet and throws a fit, they give in."
Grandmother of three

"I just want to tell them what may seem cute now will not seem so funny when their children get older." And, it is a lot harder to rein in a child's behavior when they no longer get their way by pushing parents to give in. Because they're older, smarter and have learned the lesson that if they keep pushing, it works.

Eventually, the parents will say stop and mean it. A house can be dangerous and parents have things they don't want their children to break. Still, children will keep on pushing. They will always push past the point when they start believing their parents mean it, just to see if it's true. And, if the line moves, if a parent gives in, a child will push past that line. Until they find the real line. Is this a game you really want to play?

I once attended an after-hours meeting at work. One of the mothers had brought in her two young children. Most of us were parents, so, we tolerated the toddlers' behavior. Up to a point. When they started climbing on the tables and jumping off, several of us took the children down, got paper and pens from our offices and set them up to keep them busy at an out-of-the-way desk in the room.

> *Granny-Guru's* **Grains of Wisdom: Consistent rules applied early** actually make it easier for the next step – letting up on the rules as a child gets old enough to show their own judgment.

Why didn't their mother do this?

I talked to her about it later, expecting her to be embarrassed that others had had to step in. Instead, I was astounded to hear her say, "Well, I don't really feel like I have the right to discipline them." What?! I wanted to shake her. If not her, then who? That is the mother's job. To teach her children what is acceptable behavior and what is not. The easiest place to do this is at home, where you have complete control and no distractions. But, you'd better do it by the time you take your child out in public. Sure, there are lots of parents like me who think a little crying is normal for babies and a little rambunctiousness is cute in a toddler. But, even we have a limit to our patience. Like a few minutes. Adults without children of their own have much less.

The more common reaction is, why aren't these parents controlling their children? Don't they know that it gets harder the older they get? Don't they know that the world will teach them discipline soon enough if their parents don't? How can a child be safe if they haven't learned how to stop when they are told to stop? If they haven't learned how not to break things? How can a child be successful in school if they haven't learned to sit still?

Sure, sure. Children get tired. They get pushed past their limits and you can't always take them home. But, they can learn to be quiet even when they're tired. A two-year-old has no judgment and little self-discipline. It's the parent's job to substitute their rules until a child develops his own. Even then, a child's rules are simply the parents' rules internalized. Where do you think they get them?

Do people think that what a two-year-old does has no effect on what a five-year-old will do? Habits are habits. What you are teaching your children today is how they expect the world to be. And bad habits are hard to break.

This is not just a difference of opinion about how strict to be. This is a matter of safety. Of consideration for others. Of being responsible for your children's behavior. And, yes, it's hard. But, make it easy on yourself. Teach your children the behavior you want them to have. Imagine they are still doing that cute thing as an adult. It wouldn't be so funny then. And, that is what you are teaching them now. How to be an adult. Soon enough, with your patience, they will learn the discipline that not only shows the world what good parents you are, but helps to keep your children safe.

I'd Rather Do It Myself (M)

"Say what you want to say, but then respect what I want to do. Let me make my own mistakes."
Mother of a not-quite-two-year-old

But, we could save you so much time and heartache if you'd just do it our way. Well, at least this is what Grandmothers feel, whether they say it or not. But, it's not always so.

So, how do we impart all our hard-won knowledge? Either we try to keep still because we don't want to squash the spirit of the mothers of our grandchildren, or we tell them what we know they need to hear and they don't listen!

And, what about the fact that some things really have changed? My son recently called his old walker, which I had saved, thinking to let my grandchildren use it, a "death trap." As it turns out, too many children used them near the top of stairs and fell down the stairs, with much more serious injuries than if they'd just fallen. Same with cribs, because the slats used to be far enough apart for a child's head to fit through, with disastrous consequences. Am I really being responsible by using the crib that once belonged to my husband with my precious grandchildren?

Same with baby blankets and sleeping on their tummies, now replaced by sleepers and sleeping on their backs until they can turn over themselves. Informed by analysis of risk factors for Sudden Infant Death Syndrome (SIDS). Pacifiers on strings then, clips now. Moms might feel justified in ignoring old advice from a different time.

But, not all advice is outdated. Supporting a newborn's head doesn't seem to be taught anymore. Either the crook of your arm or your hand under its neck and head. My Mom taught me this when I was in elementary school and we were visiting a new neighbor's baby. Learning how to avoid or treat diaper rash. I learned about sunlight from my Mom. Cold water for burns. My husband learned this working at a grill.

Mothers are asking for two things. First, allow for the fact that there may be new information available that drives their decisions, and we need to respect that. Second, they may not do everything right. We certainly did not. But, some things cannot be told; they have to be tried. No child would learn to walk if we surrounded them with pillows to soften their falls. A mother deserves the same emotional space to make her own mistakes. After all, she is going to have to live with the consequences, just as we did. She deserves not only our respect, but, our confidence in her judgment and her ability to recognize and correct her own mistakes. We cannot be the pillows to soften all those falls. But, we can tell stories.

> *Granny-Guru*'s **Grains of Wisdom: Correction is not respect; it suggests a lack of confidence in another adult to make their own decisions – even when you are right☺ Do things** with your grandchildren in your home that show how you do things. She will either copy and learn from them, or ignore them, according to her own best judgment.

Learn more about the Back-to-Sleep campaign at our blog post: http://newgrandmas.com/backtosleep

Don't Touch My Dresser! (M)

"When my children were young, my Mom used to come visit and I kept catching her in my bedroom, neatly arranging, spreading out and dusting all the perfumes and lotions on my dresser. I'm sure she thought she was doing me a favor."
Mother of a son and daughter, now in high school and college

"But, I knew everything was now within reach and as soon as my toddlers came in they would take them all down. I immediately pushed them all to the back of the dresser as soon as I saw it."

Apparently, this Grandmother forgot, not only the 10-foot reach of toddlers, but, their curiosity and inability to distinguish breakables from toys.

Childproofing isn't just covering up the electrical outlets. It is looking at your house with a toddler's eyes. I once gave my son an old iron to play with, thinking he could no longer hurt it, and it might spur his curiosity about how things work. My husband, horrified, caught him as he was preparing to put loose wires in a nearby outlet.

My other son once gave himself away as a toddler when I heard him in my mother-in-law's bedroom saying, "No, no, no." When I rushed in to see what he was up to, he was standing on her bench, looking over her jewelry box, still saying, "No, no, no." He got the

Granny-Guru's Grains of Wisdom: Grandmas just want to help. They know they are loved, but irrelevant. And, they remember being relevant in your life. It's a good feeling that is worth trying to recapture. And, can't we all use a little spoiling?

concept but not the point. He knew he wasn't supposed to be in her jewelry box, but, in an unguarded moment, curiosity overcame him.

When our children were young, we had wooden cubes as coffee tables. They were indestructible. We briefly had a marble coffee table, until our son fell into it and cracked his head. My parents had given it to us when they remodeled. We quickly gave it back. The furniture adults choose when they are surrounded by adults is not the furniture the parents of young children might choose.

Grandmothers might remember similar stories about their own children, but forget what it means. Histories are overlaid with the many and more recent memories of children who have learned judgment and restraint acting with the care of adults

So, what's a mother to do? She can't be expected to follow around after her mother as she would her own children. Perhaps a conversations and stories would be helpful to re-orient the grandmother to the dangers facing curious toddlers. As in, "I don't let my children play with my perfumes, because they don't know how to handle them carefully yet. That is why they are pushed out of reach, at the back of my dresser." And, then, because Grandma is just trying to help, to be useful, to do something special for her daughter, some suggestions about what she can do.

"You know, Mom, I've got scented drawer liner paper that I never can get around to cutting to fit my drawers. It would be wonderful if you felt like doing something special for me, if you could do that. I would thank you every time I opened my drawers." Or match the socks, or sew on a button. This same Mom remembers her own Mom having to-do lists when grandparents visited. Grandpa hung pictures and fixed squeaky chairs. Grandma cleaned everything in the china cabinet and baked Christmas cookies. The things you wish you had time to do.

Don't Be So Afraid (G)

"Your children need to learn how to make their own decisions. It is dangerous to try to protect them from everything."
   Mother of two, Grandmother of two

A baby gate to keep a four-year-old off the stairs? Most families give up on baby gates shortly after their children reach the age of two because they can either unlatch them or climb over them. Climbing on bales of hay, under supervision, is prohibited? What if they did fall? Would a broken arm be the end of the world? More likely, they won't. And, what fun to climb around on soft bales of hay with a bunch of other children.

When does reasonable fear become obsessive? How do you balance safety and independence? When do children get to start learning lessons on their own about how to be in the world? I once read a chilling story, don't know if it was true, about a rich man's son who was so carefully watched that, at the age of ten, when he slipped through a garden gate, unobserved, he walked into a street and was killed by a car. He had no idea that he needed to look out for them.

This isn't what we want for our children. What we want is that balance that comes from protecting them when they are infants and completely vulnerable, to loosening the restraints gradually, as appropriate for their age.

> *Granny-Guru*'s **Grains of Wisdom. There's fear. And, there's unreasonable fear.** But, when will the children learn that independence of judgment that will protect them when Mom's not there?

But, what's the other side? When is it time to let go? How much, how soon? If parents know their children better than anyone, aren't they the ones to decide what their children can handle? Sometimes parents need to learn that balance.

Where is the middle ground? Children appropriately using their judgment, while not taking unnecessary risks. This is where the norms of books can be helpful. I remember reading in a Dr. Brazelton book[13], years ago, that, on average, infants cry five or six hours a day. And, it's not all bad. They are building lung capacity. My children didn't cry nearly that much, but, it certainly relieved my concern about them, and about my parenting.

Little People: Guidelines for Common Sense Child Rearing,[14] is one of those normative books, like Dr. Brazelton in my day, but meant for children beyond the toddler years. He makes the point that children learn how to act in the world through independent play. By imagining something, then making it. It is the physical act of putting something together, building something that gives them the confidence that they can control their world. Much of how children come to understand the world comes from moving around in it, exploring.

It does not matter whether the world really is more dangerous or whether we are simply aware of more dangers. My children were never allowed to eat Halloween candy they collected without my inspecting it first. Who could have imagined, as happened in my day, that someone would put razor blades in apples they gave to children? Children don't get apples for Halloween anymore, or even homemade candy. Only store-bought, individually wrapped candy. Or, more often, only candy they get at organized parties, not trick-or-treating at strangers' homes. So, good parenting means appropriate care.

---

[13] Get the book, *Touchpoints: Birth to Three*, T. Berry Brazelton, MD here: http://newgrandmas.com/touchpoints

[14] Get the book, *Little People*, by Dr. Edward R. Christophersen, here: http://newgrandmas.com/littlepeople

But, it also means age-appropriate hands-off to let children be. I was recently told that one young mother felt the criticism of her neighbors when she let her children play alone at a near-by creek. They had cell phones, of course. But, they were playing alone. Why wasn't she afraid for them? She wasn't afraid for them because they were near home in a safe neighborhood. And, she felt it was more important for them to have some unsupervised time to play. They're children.

The National Center for Missing and Exploited Children reports that while 797,500 children are reported missing every year, 115 of these fall into what is considered 'stereotypical kidnapping,' that is, kidnapping by a stranger with an intent to keep or harm.[15][16]

No risk is acceptable when it is your child. But, a sense of balance and the real danger is also appropriate. After all, we are also trying to teach our children the self-confidence that comes from trying things on your own. Creating things that no one has ever thought of before.

It begins at play. It begins with incremental, age-appropriate, managed risk taking. Even for a four-year-old.

---

[15] Statistics on missing children. http://www.missingkids.com/missingkids/servlet/PageServlet?LanguageCountry=en_US&PageId=2810

[16] What to do if your child is missing. http://www.klaaskids.org/pg-mc-whattodo.htm

Because I'm the Mom, That's Why (M)

"Mountain Dew has more caffeine than Coke, Diego 'fruit snacks' aren't fruit and the charms from Lucky Charms are not appropriate for an 18-month-old's breakfast."
  Mother of a two-and-a-half-year-old & nearly-one-year-old

As this particular child started life with baby acid reflux that kept him awake every hour or two throughout the night, and still has allergies that require a medicinal regimen to regulate, food choices are not just a responsible attempt to keep sugar at bay as long as possible. Rather, they are recognition of the difference healthy food choices make in their child's life.

Sugar, caffeine, allergies. Parents are much more aware of their effects today than we were. The scare with Red Dye #2 was the first food-related incident I remember that changed the way parents looked at the foods their children were eating.

> *Granny-Guru's* **Grains of Wisdom:** Help her out. Pay attention. **I'm not going to tell you again.** Stock up on fruit. Milk or water to drink. You'd rather they spend money on college, not dentists. (No offense to my dentist friends and cousins ☺) And, don't argue.

A suspected carcinogen, it was banned by the FDA in 1976, and Mars withdrew red M&M™'s even though they didn't use that dye. Still, I tried to keep sugar out of my younger son's diet as long as possible, too. Because I knew that where sugar goes, cavities soon follow. And, I couldn't bear the thought of those beautiful baby teeth being marred by cavities. Experts, by then, had determined that cavities in baby teeth were something to be concerned about, because they could change the position of where permanent teeth came in. Before then, the thinking was, well, they're baby teeth. They'll be replaced anyway.

But, I remember the day I lost the battle. I put sugar on my cereal in the kitchen, usually out-of-sight of my son eating breakfast in the dining room. This day he saw me. "What are you putting on your cereal, Mommy?" And, of course, since children want to do what their parents do, eat what their parents eat, he wanted sugar on his cereal too. I wasn't willing to give it up then, though I don't use it now. Similarly, I rarely allowed him tea and never coffee. But, those rules really tightened up one evening when my husband asked if our son had had any caffeine that day. Well, yes. I had let him have a sip of my iced tea at lunch. The effects were obvious hours later. That ended even that modest practice.

Even raisins, which I thought healthy, a pediatric dentist friend told me were the worst possible food. Because they are sticky, they keep the sugar on the teeth. Update to today's fruit snacks.

So, let's assume these grandparents are trying to be the good guys. They want their grandchildren to remember visits with them fondly, as this young mother remembers daily visits with her grandmother. But, they don't get to see their grandchildren daily. So, their choices of how to build those memories tend to the easy joys. Sugar. Caffeine. What could it hurt? I treat all my grandchildren the same way.

Except, your grandchildren are not all the same. And, their mothers are not all the same. What you might consider over-mothering, she considers appropriate health-consciousness. What you might consider excessive attention to detail, she believes is responsible parenting.

It's not a reflection on you, really. Lists of details about a child's daily routine do not mean you're an idiot. They are guidelines, designed to alert you to what this child is used to. One of the advantages, after all, of going to Grandma and Grandpa's is to learn that things can be done differently. But, food sensitivities aren't to be ignored.

You've raised your children successfully, so, you've already won. This is a different contest. Her rules are now in play. And, yes, you may be indulging extra caution in the name of good parenting. But, you love her.

Your Son is Not Perfect! (M)

"Your son is not perfect!"
    Mother of a 2-year-old and 4-year-old

Yes, he is. And, so are you, in the eyes of your father. It's all a matter of where you stand when you are looking.

When our sons were born, they were perfect. With our loving guidance, we have raised them up to be self-sufficient, kind, honest, and good with children – all the qualities you wanted in a husband. We tried to give them the foundation for developing a good partnership with a good woman, and the judgment to find one. It worked. They found you.

But, we no longer live with them from day-to-day. And, even when we did, it was never in an equal partnership. We always had the upper hand. Still do. If we ask for something really important, we can usually get it.

But, we have to be careful what we ask for. Because, now, his primary loyalty is to you. That is as it should be. And, your responsibility is to treat him like an adult. Someone who is expected to shoulder their responsibility for earning a living, raising children, and keeping each other happy.

> *Granny-Guru*'s **Grains of Wisdom: Husbands and wives set the rules of their relationship**. All a grandmother really wants is to hear stories she can use to brag on her son and grandchildren to her friends and pretend she still matters in his life, knowing that it is really his wife who matters now.

Negotiating the details of those responsibilities lies squarely between the two of you. That is why you think he is not perfect.

Your son is not perfect!

You see him as human. You keep him grounded. You do not let him get too discouraged when things in the real world are not going well, or too smug when they are. And, he does the same for you.

A mother's unconditional love for her son is not the same as a wife's conditional love for her husband. Neither is stronger or better. They are just different. And, they fill different roles in our lives. A mother may try to re-create the feelings of her loving relationship with her son by remembering that he likes brownies or licorice or coconut in an attempt to re-connect to the time when she was important in his daily life. A wife can re-create some of those memories to honor her husband's wishes and satisfy his tastes, but, more importantly, she creates new memories together with her husband and children that underline the fact that they have created a new, unique home together. A daughter-in-law and mother-in-law do not serve each other well by trying to compete over creating this warm feeling.

And, that is why we can keep our illusion that he is perfect. We do not live in the real world with him. We see him as the grown-up version of that perfect baby we have loved all these years.

Just like your Daddy sees you.

The TV is Not a Babysitter (M)

"This is a shout out to Grandpa. Sticking my children in front of TV is not considered babysitting."
    Mother of a toddler and a near-toddler

What does a grandfather have in common with children under the age of three? What in the world can they do? They can barely talk. They want to do everything on their own, but they can't do much of anything without help. They are moving all the time, and you never know if they're going to get into something dangerous. Professional athletes, in a study to see just how active two-year-olds really are, could not keep up with them. How can a grandparent?!

And, young children get frustrated easily. Are they tired? Hungry? Homesick? They're in-between that age when they are almost ready to go to the bathroom themselves, but you still have to keep an eye out for signs that they need to but haven't told you yet.

Oh, let's just let them watch TV. Then, we know they'll be happy and safe. What's the harm?

Fifty years later and we're still trying to figure out the best way to use television. I ignored the violence in Saturday morning cartoons so my husband and I could sleep in when our children were young. Studies told us that watching newscasts was actually worse for children. At least they knew the violence on cartoons wasn't real. And, they liked Sesame Street, a teaching tool before home schooling was popular.

> **Granny-Guru's Grains of Wisdom: Make the effort**. Don't give the time up to television. Which doesn't make memories the way only you can. Television can't teach you to whistle.

According to the American Academy of Pediatrics, children under the age of two should not watch any television, computer screens or videos. This zero-tolerance guideline stretches to an hour or two a day for older children, though the average actually watched is four.[17] Too much television has been linked to obesity in older children and is suspected for retarding brain development in younger children. So, it can cause harm. Real, long-lasting harm. And, like candy, though occasional visits with grandparents may seem like they won't cause any damage, they set a child up to pressure parents once they get home. Parents have to pick their fights. Don't give them more battles to fight.

What should Grandpa be doing with his precious grandchildren? Reading to them, of course. Including them in hobbies, where possible. Gardening, as long as you don't expect to get too much done with all that help. Fishing. Worms. Grasshoppers. Bird watching. There is even a great book to match up recorded bird songs with the ones you see on your bird feeder, called *Bird Songs: 250 North American Birds in Song*.[18]

Playing a penny whistle. Our grandson could start playing by the time he was two after watching Grandpa. Walking around the neighborhood, showing off your precious grandchildren. Everyone in our church knows our grandchildren, even though we only take them a few times a year. Ditto the farmers' market, which has a parked train to climb on next door. Do you have something that needs to be stacked? My grandson and I stacked logs for the woodstove; the small ones were the perfect length and weight for his strength. Are there paper airplanes that need to be flown? Bubbles that need to be blown? Balls that need to be tossed?

---

[17] Discussion on the effects of television on children. http://kidshealth.org/parent/positive/family/tv_affects_child.html
[18] Get the book, *Bird Songs*, here: http://newgrandmas.com/birdsongs

One creative grandfather taught his three grandchildren, ranging in age from three to seven, how to make home-made no-knead, slow-rise bread, and made a video to show the rest of us how it's done.[19]

It's precious, this little time we have with grandchildren. We know they will grow up all too soon. And, all too soon, it will be harder to have them come visit. They will have friends to play with, schoolwork to do, jobs to go to. Only now, when they are too young to be companions, are they available to grandparents long out of the habit of playing with children.

Check out our website for the series of interviews with pediatrician and Assistant Professor of Pediatrics at the University of Alabama, at Birmingham, and mother of a 13-month-old and 3-year-old, Dr. Amanda Soong.

Grandparents flunked when she asked them about current recommendations for childhood safety and nutrition. Find out what's recommended now! http://newgrandmas.com. Search on Soong

---

[19] Bread made in Bed – The Grandkids Sequel video
http://www.youtube.com/watch?v=sQQOeP14P_4

Grandmothers Who Date (M)

"I helped my Mom set up her online profiles for a dating site. But, I drew the line at letting her take our toddler daughter on a blind date with someone she'd only known for a week. She thinks I have too many rules."
Mother of two daughters under four

Dating again after more than thirty years of marriage must be scary. You're not only not young anymore, you don't hang out where single people hang out. So, where do you meet them? The usual advice is church, clubs with people of shared interests, adult classes, the grocery store. Neighborhoods filled with families can be nervous about unattached singles in their midst. Friends will try to fix you up. If you're in your twenties or thirties, Parents without Partners. But, what if your children are grown?

Out of the dating pool since I was nineteen, I listen curiously to the many friends who met their now spouses online. And, they are perfectly happy. And, their spouses are perfectly normal. So, it can be done, and apparently, this is how it's being done now. This young mother not only approves of her Mom's efforts, she is helping her navigate the unfamiliar online world. But.

Now, I'm no expert. I get my sense of today's culture from watching *Friends*, *How I Met Your Mother*, and the like. But, it seems to me, a common thread in shows depicting Moms newly single shows them uncommonly reluctant to introduce their children to dates, for all the reasons this Mom objects. Revolving boyfriends is the wrong message to send to children. It is disruptive and confusing. This Mom's young daughter was confused that she wasn't going to have the same teacher in her 3-year-old pre-school class that she had in her 2-year-old pre-school class.

Adults, no matter whether they are trying or not, are modeling behavior for children. I once volunteered with a program that was designed around that premise. Young volunteer mothers were paired with young mothers who had been brought to the attention of social services because they abused or neglected their children. They were only allowed to enter the program if they stopped the abuse. But, mostly, they were mothers with poor parenting skills. The idea was to let them hang out with mothers with normal parenting skills, to see how it was done. And, we did not teach them anything about how to be a parent. We were just there to be friends. As we each had our children with us, the modeling behavior was a natural fall-out.

This Grandmother may think she is just involving her grandchildren in her new life. But, she seems to be using them as protection in a scary world, as she implicitly says to her dates, "Yes, I'm old enough to have grandchildren, but, aren't they lovely."

> *Granny-Guru*'s **Grains of Wisdom: Moms get to draw the line on who their children meet.** Grandparents entering a world of new friends need to shield their grandchildren from this world until new friends become old friends.

As scary as that dating world is, you don't get to use your grandchildren as a shield. Take pictures with you instead.

Chapter 3
Elementary School

Don't Yell at the Children! (G)

"I told my daughter I could hear her yelling from the garden. She just got mad at me. Sure, raising one child is not the same as raising three, but yelling doesn't seem to work, either."
Grandmother of three, mother of one

A yelling mother is a frustrated mother. It means she has reached the end of her patience. Used in small doses, it can signal to a child, that's the end of excuses. You had better do it now or get in real trouble. Children are masters at figuring out what our codes are. They watch our behavior. So, if yelling just means more nagging, but at a higher pitch, it can be ignored as easily as the nagging.

Observing this cycle of nagging, then yelling, with no change in behavior from the children who are the object of it, can be very frustrating. It also carries the risk that when this Mom really wants to get her children's attention, she won't be able to. They will be used to ignoring her.

In this case, the grandmother did something different, once she realized that her nagging about yelling was having the same effect on the mother of her grandchildren as the yelling did on the grandchildren. She changed course. She told the mother about a book she had read that suggested when you really want to get your child's attention, you lower your voice instead of raising it. This has the advantage that the children have to stop and struggle to hear what is being said. But, it also has the advantage that the parent is consciously controlling their reaction, instead of falling back on the more natural yelling. And, that control is going to get a child's attention every time.

I found out once, when I had laryngitis and my son was about three, that I could keep him within range of a whisper in a store. I had to, because I could not yell to bring him back to where I was shopping. And, it turned out to be a lot easier than I would have thought. Children adjust to us. It's a survival behavior for them. It is up to us to decide how we want to use this advantage.

Don't let yelling be the normal way you keep your children in line. The normal way is consistent boundaries consistently enforced. "No, you know you can't have a snack before dinner. It will spoil your appetite." The first, sixth and twentieth time they ask. They'll get tired of asking as long as the answer remains the same. And, the need for yelling will go down over time. "I don't care what your friends do. I'm not going to let you do it." "I don't care what Grandma lets you do, in our house we don't do that."

> *Granny-Guru*'s **Grains of Wisdom: Don't yell at the children.** Sure, there will always be times. But, save that level of urgency for when you really need it. Or when you're telling your children, you've just used up my last thread of patience. And, that doesn't happen every day.

BTW, this same grandmother said she had wonderful grandparents, who gave her a core sense of self-esteem from the love they heaped on her. The mother of her grandchildren says her grandparents gave her that same feeling. This grandmother hopes her grandchildren get that same comfort from her love. It's pretty clear she's looking out for them.

Don't Treat My Children Different (M)

"You may not share the same interests with both children, or personality. But, please treat them both the same."
Mother of two girls

Recently, a gentleman, with tears in his eyes, told me that his grandmother had not liked boys. He remembered vividly the conversation one night after dinner, when he reached for a second helping of custard pie. His grandmother spoke sharply to his mother, "Are you going to let that boy have another piece of pie?!" His mother, defending him, said, "He's a growing boy. He can have all the pie he wants."

Children may not notice a difference in treatment, unless it is pointed and physically obvious, as it was for that boy, or if grandparents favor one child with a different number of presents at Christmas, or presents more often, or always go to or greet one child before the other. Children, after all, unless confronted with differences they cannot ignore, are likely to assume their grandparents love them equally, as they probably do, no matter how they show it. Mothers, however, are acutely aware if grandparents treat any of their children differently. Because, mothers appreciate all the different talents their children have, not just the more social ones some may excel in.

As far as I could tell, my grandparents treated us all the same. We were all featured on the annual videos my grandfather took and showed off to all the family as he made the annual trek to each of his far-flung children's homes. We all got presents every Christmas. And, I never remember comparing notes when the cousins got together. Simple fairness was also a family principle we lived by. That is not to say we didn't all also have our own place in the family. I was the only girl. One brother the oldest child. One the youngest.

But, the absurdity of how carefully my parents tried to treat us the same came home to me when my mother came to live with us after a debilitating stroke. The subject of peas came up. I've always disliked them. But, I bragged to my husband one evening that our parents were so careful to treat us all the same that we all had to eat the same serving of peas when they came up in the vegetable rotation, though none of us liked them. My mother, words chosen carefully after having recovered a bit of speech, suddenly proclaimed, "Only you."

I didn't believe her. Was she saying I was the only one who didn't like peas? I called my brothers immediately. Laughing, they confessed, that, yes, they liked peas! Now how fair is that?! I would happily have given them mine! I did not bother to ask if there was a vegetable they did not like that I did, to even things out.

> *Granny-Guru*'s **Grains of Wisdom: When a loving and loved adult in a child's life favors one child in a family, the least they can do is mask that by showing equal attention to all the children.** Because such favor hides the fact that they really do love all their grandchildren. They just may not know how to show it equally.

And, that's the rub. Parents try to treat children equally, even, though, of course, children are not the same. And, they ask, in the name of instilling this principle in their children, that grandparents do the same.

Grandma's House. Grandma's Rules. (G)

"I try to respect the rules set for my grandchildren by their parents. Just like my husband and I tried to create a united front in raising our children. But, when I see those kids out on the street barefoot, I have a fit."
    Grandmother of three grandsons

"Put on your flip-flops, at least. Don't make me have a heart attack. You have to play quietly here. I live in a senior living community. And, you know that is a word I don't like to hear. I do ask the children, 'What is your mother's position on this?' if I think they might be trying to get away with something. I try to follow her guidelines, but whatever I can get away with that makes the kids smile, full-speed ahead."

And, that is exactly the dilemma, isn't it? The advantage and disadvantage to the fact that we do not see our grandchildren every day. We want every visit to be special. We are not paying lip service to the idea of reinforcing parents' rules. We believe in it. We understand deeply from the experience of holding the line on discipline with our own children how important it is to support those rules. How difficult and tiring for parents to shoulder the whole burden of enforcement.

And, there's our wish to be a little protective. While we love the idea of rambunctious boys, we are years removed from the reality. And, our circumstances have changed. From the single family home our children remember to shared space with seniors who may not welcome the joyful noise of boys.

> *Granny-Guru's* **Grains of Wisdom: Grandma's house. Grandma's rules.** Adults simply do not handle the world the same way. What a gift for grandchildren to find this out from the adults who love them most.

But, those smiles. Our joy and our reward. Physical evidence that we have succeeded in the game of life. How could there be anything wrong with trying to get more smiles? This grandmother understands that even very young children can sort out the fact that just because you get to do it at home does not mean you will get to do it at Grandma's house. And, she hopes they can also sort out the fact that just because you get to do it at Grandma's house does not mean you will get to do it at home. Another mother said tension went down in her house when they instituted the Las Vegas rule. What happens at Grandma's house stays at Grandma's house.

This Grandma keeps in close touch with phone calls between visits. Routinely brings educational toys and games as small gifts. Even turning t-shirts from around the world into a wider learning and sharing conversation.

She understands that children learn from the modeling behavior of adults. So, she has a library full of books. A piano to be played. Crystal and china for proper occasions. Does not use candy to get those smiles. But, the lives of grandchildren at Grandma's house. This is the time to make memories.

Why Do You Ignore Your Grandchildren? (M)

"Except for Christmas and birthdays, she seems not to be interested in her grandchildren."
            Mother of two

"Phone calls. Notes. Small reminders that you are thinking about them. Don't you care? Aren't you interested?"

Since we start with the assumption that all Grandmothers love their grandchildren, why would a young mother get the impression the Grandmother of her children is not interested? Sure, there's the distance problem. If you are not within driving distance of a grandchild's family, trips can be expensive and planned rarely. But, there may simply be a difference in expectations. What is meant by being a good Grandmother?
Some might think that remembering holidays with presents is enough. This Mother clearly feels a longing for a closer relationship and does not believe that distance is an excuse.

But, what is the Grandmother thinking? Does she not have a close relationship with the Mother of her grandchildren? Is she loathe to interfere, afraid that closer contact would be seen as intrusive? Does her culture suggest an emotional distance she has never questioned? Is she more comfortable with children who are older than her grandchildren?

> *Granny-Guru*'s **Grains of Wisdom: It is possible to train someone to live closer to your expectations for communicating.** Millennials may expect more contact more often than Boomers, but that is not the only reason there are missed opportunities for expressions of love.

My mother, for instance, never really got involved in her grandchildren's lives until they were in junior high. She had them for a week every summer and saw them every Christmas, but she really started warming up to them when they were closer to having adult interests. She arranged for a neighbor's child, a few years older, to take one grandchild to one of the large amusement parks near by and she took him with her on rounds as a volunteer at a local hospital. She dropped off her other grandson at the foot of the Appalachian Trail for a hike another summer.

She loved showing them off to her friends, carried pictures of them with her, and bragged about them to anyone who would listen. But, this only got back to us when we happened to talk to her friends. Her way was to let compliments come back indirectly. Telling us such things, I suppose, would have seemed obvious or insincere. A pattern I should have recognized from her own parenting style. She did not compliment us directly, but delightedly told us about compliments friends had given her about us.

Someone once taught me that the way to get more communication is to initiate it. This Grandmother may be waiting for the chance to show her love, may be clueless that she isn't, or, may indeed not be interested. There are certainly Grandmothers who believe that they have finished the job of raising their own children and are no longer very interested in children, even their own grandchildren. I'd bet on clueless.

When Are You Going to Start Feeding Those Children Properly? (G)

"Orange instead of apple juice. Oatmeal instead of cookie cereal. Real food instead of junk."
2 boys, 2 girls, 9 grandchildren

This grandmother might be a little more sensitive about diet these days, as she fights cancer. She took it upon herself to dig deeper than the advice doctors were giving her and find a dietician who specialized in her situation.

Lots of fruits and vegetables, of course. Reduced meat. Avoid alcohol, of course. Cut out sugar. Cut out sugar?! Do you know how hard that is when you're around grandchildren?!

I tried to cut out sugar a few years ago, when I went on the No White Food diet to drop a few pounds. I was told later it was not endorsed by the Mayo Clinic, as I had understood. But, it was easy to follow. No potatoes or rice. No white bread. No cheese. No dairy. No sugar. My husband eventually convinced me that whole grain rice was ok, since the point was to eat whole grains, not the too easily metabolized, starchy potatoes or polished white rice I was used to. He started cooking whole grain rice and looking for other grains – barley, amaranth, teff, wheat berries, bulgur. It got to be a game to see how many new whole grains he could find.

> *Granny-Guru*'s **Grains of Wisdom: The 1950s may have been where America really started to buy into the processed food lifestyle.** Now the choice is between processed food and fast food. Or, a simple, homemade dinner.

When are you going to start feeding that child properly?

I never ate much white bread, rarely ate sandwiches. Eventually, my husband figured out how to make bread with whole grains, so we could feel pretty righteous. I actually eat much more bread now than I used to, hot, fresh bread as soon as it comes out of the bread machine or oven, made with a spoonful of honey. Homemade toast at dinner with olive oil, sprinkled with rosemary from the backyard if I'm feeling ambitious. Yumm.

I switched to oatmeal, first with brown sugar, then honey, then nothing but warm milk.

When I was cooking for my Mom at my brother's house, in the last five weeks of her life, I learned how easy it is to put out a meal for five, even if you have no cookbooks. 45-50 minutes from door to table to roast a chicken and vegetables (carrots, potatoes, onions, butternut squash) while you are doing other things. Sandwiches, salad and soup to follow. Cheap. Healthy. Low fat. Salmon steak slathered with olive oil and dill, baked in a toaster oven. Sweet potatoes baked in the microwave. Fresh asparagus microwaved for five minutes and topped with butter. Fresh fruit salad of pineapple, tumbled with apple and pear, no dressing. Ice water to drink. 15-20 minutes. All goodness.

No sugar. That one's been a lot harder. For one thing, it's in everything. Toothpaste?! Turns out, it used to be illegal to add sugar to beer, a cheap way to speed up the fermentation process. Not any more, of course. Any processed food is likely to have sugar in it. It may have started out as a preservative, but now, it's everywhere. And, for a second thing, I love it. I used to keep candy in my desk. I'd share with people who came to visit, but I always had it available. I thought of myself as a junk food queen. Sugar is a hard habit to break.

So, what's the answer for these grandchildren? How to convince their mothers they need to pay attention? If the cost of fillings hasn't penetrated yet, it will. It's not inevitable. It's a direct result of sugar. And, processed food.

We know. All the health food books say the same thing. Buy food around the edges of the grocery store. The food that is raw and healthy. The food you cook yourself. Not the food that comes in cans and boxes. It takes a little more time to get something ready for dinner. But, this is one of those, pay me now, or pay me later lessons.

Frisk Your Mother for Candy (M)

"I told my boyfriend he has to frisk his mother before she's allowed in. She keeps bringing Jolly Ranchers hard candies even though we've asked her not to."
      Mother of four sons and three stepchildren

Where are the boundaries? When is it innocent treats and when does it become defying the mother of your grandchildren? We grandmothers laugh at the idea that we can't bring our grandchildren candy, knowing that their parents will have to deal with the sugar high it brings after we've gone home. But, parents these days are much more serious about restricting sugar than when our children were young. When I was growing up, I spent my allowance every week at the candy shop three blocks from my house. When we were raising our children, we were just starting to learn the relationship between sugar and cavities.

Since then, we've come to know much more about sugar and hyperactivity and parents are much more likely to control sweets. While I remember the horror of watching one young mother routinely give her child sweet drinks even from the age of two, and seeing the inevitable result when he had cavities by the age of five, I was much less aware of the behavior effect of sugar. With my first son, I never thought much about sending in cookies or brownies for classroom treats. When I gave my second son frozen peas for teething, other parents thought I was being conscientious, but they didn't copy me. But, by the time he was playing soccer, oranges were the routine half-time treat, and toys had slipped into Halloween trick-or-treat bags to replace some of the candy. Today, carrots and bananas are as likely to be a snack provided for children at group activities as cookies.

> *Granny-Guru's* **Grains of Wisdom**. It is not what you bring them; it is how you expand their world to include yours that makes memories.

Frisk Your Mother for Candy

Yet, grandmothers are not really trying to be subversive. We are trying to be someone our grandchildren look forward to seeing.

It's a cheap trick, candy. Yet, it is a high no less than sugar to see the delight on their faces. When our time with them is a limited privilege, we think we can build happy memories by building a tie between the generations that leaps over the barrier that we are out-of-touch with almost everything else in their lives. Their clothes, their toys, what and how they study at school, their friends, even their parents' rules are something we cannot keep up with because it is no longer part of our daily lives.

So, what are the choices? My mother used to collect toy prizes when she won something at a bridge game or found a toy in a cereal box to give our children when they visited. One young mother suggested setting up a theme that captures your interest and giving grandchildren toys around that theme and building in activities to share – gardening, a particular kind of doll with its accessories, books, fishing, sailing, cooking. I remember listening in fascination when a great-aunt told me about having lunch with the princess of Japan. As a missionary, she had taught English to one of her ladies-in-waiting. This aunt had given me a kimono on one visit, taught me Origami on another and inspired my interest in Asia. I eventually earned a degree in Chinese studies and keep squares of paper in my purse to make origami cranes for children in my path.

Back Off! (G)

"Back off. Give your children a chance to make their own mistakes. Don't hover over them every minute."
   Grandmother of three

They're now called "helicopter parents." [20] Although Wikipedia refers to the term in the context of parents being over-involved after a child leaves for college (calling to wake them up for class?!), I saw the beginnings of it when my younger son was in Cub Scouts. Parents making the cars for Pinewood Derby, apparently in an effort to help their son know what it felt like to win. Well, of course, the car made by an adult was going to beat the car made by a 10-year-old. But, what did that teach children? Parents cheat? When I challenged a parent about what I considered unfair competition, he sheepishly admitted, "Well, I let him paint it." How satisfying is it for a child to win when he did not even make the car?

I recently attended a Leadership seminar on the differences between managing the Boomer generation and the Millennial generation[21], led by Misti Burmeister, CEO of Inspirion, Inc., and author of *From Boomers to Bloggers: Success Strategies Across Generations*. Her mission is to improve communications across generations[22]. She described one frustrated Boomer manager who said he told a new Millennial hire the outlines of a job that needed to be done and pointed them vaguely at the resources needed to do it. This is a common test for new hires, who are expected to show they have enough initiative to figure

---

[20] http://en.wikipedia.org/wiki/Helicopter_parent
[21] Boomers are considered to be those born between the years 1946 and 1964. Generation X or GenX between 1965 and 1980. Generation Y or Millennials between 1980 and 1994
[22] Get the book, *From Boomers to Bloggers*, here: http://newgrandmas.com/boomerstobloggers

out how to get a job done. But, in this case, the new hire kept going back to the manager, asking for direction. Frustrated, the manager finally burst out, "Do you want me to do the job for you?!" Later, I was talking to one of the Millennials in the room. He said he understood the story perfectly, and now better understood some of the feedback he was getting from his managers.

The point of the seminar was to inform Boomer managers that this generation is used to being constantly in touch. With each other, with parents. And, naturally, they expect that kind of close communication at work. The Boomer manager drew the line when parents came in with their children for the first day of work and called the manager after the first performance appraisal. Boomer managers are shocked at this kind of behavior, believing it indicates poor emotional maturity on the part of their new hires. New hires do not even understand how it could be any different, acculturated to it all their lives.

Our seminar leader, a Millennial herself, trying to bridge the generation gap for managers, pointed out that this generation is considered the brightest, most creative, most technically proficient and most socially mature ever. So, the markers that Boomer managers use to judge maturity need to be informed by this fact. But, there is also a serious reality check when Millennials are expected to act on their own initiative, without waiting for prompting by someone else. Parents, beware. When do you want your children to learn this? When they are under your roof? When they go to college, or when they go to work?

> *Granny-Guru*'s **Grains of Wisdom: Life gives feedback.** Parents can't, nor should they protect a child from all of it. Where to draw that boundary of when to step in to prevent mistakes and when to allow a child to learn from life will always be a parent's challenge.

ADHD Is An Explanation, Not An Excuse (G)

"Just because your child has some kind of physical or mental challenge, don't make that the excuse why they can't do normal things."
                          Grandmother of two

ADHD (Attention-Deficit Hyperactivity Disorder[23])? Oh, they can't be expected to sit still in class long enough to learn the lesson. Learning disability? Oh, they can't be expected to turn in a writing assignment like everyone else. The list is endless.

There is a big difference between accommodating a physical or mental challenge and using it as a get-out-of-everything card. And, it is harmful to set a child's expectations to be that they cannot perform normal tasks because of their disability. What gives them the incentive to try? How does anyone know how much that challenge really keeps them from everyday tasks? Are there workarounds? And, what does that constant reminder say to the child about their ability to manage their own lives in this world?

The Washington Post profiled a journalist a few years ago who found out as an adult that he had a serious learning disability. Experts he interviewed for the article said he never should have

Granny-Guru's **Grains of Wisdom: Don't let excuses become crutches.** ADHD [substitute relevant condition] is an explanation, not an excuse. If allowed to substitute for your own hard work, if convinced it will keep you from living life to the fullest, that belief will act as its own self-limiting barrier, not the challenge that started it.

---
[23] http://en.wikipedia.org/wiki/ADHD

been able to be a writer. A professional journalist! He had, of course, developed coping strategies to get around his difficulties growing up. And, no one told him he could not do it. How can anyone know how hard it is for someone else to learn something. School is hard. You have to work at it. Giving a child excuses does them no favors.

Still, understanding their challenges and the fact that not everyone faces those challenges might help them understand themselves a little better. I once had a piano teacher, a scientist in a previous life, who had tried for years to convince one of her children that she was, indeed, very smart. An undetected learning disability so discouraged the child that she could not think of any other explanation for her academic failures than stupidity. Finally, a year or so after she dropped out of school, her persistent mother found a test that revealed the disability. "See, I told you you were smart," the triumphant mother claimed. The child returned for a GED[24], ego restored.

Stephen Hawking, author of *A Brief History of Time*, credits his illness, in which he is confined to a wheelchair with limited movement, with his ability to focus on science and some of the great breakthroughs of our generation. It is attitude, he claims, the decision to aim at a goal that goes beyond or around the challenges you face, and the understanding that there are others worse off that can keep you going in the face of severe disability.[25] Let that be the model for conquering the world.

---

[24] General Educational Development tests, recognized as the equivalent of a high school diploma http://en.wikipedia.org/wiki/GED

[25] http://www.hawking.org.uk/disable/dindex.html

Ice Cream is Not a Meal! (M)

"Ice cream is not a meal! You never raised us this way! What is it? Does some button get pushed when you become a grandmother!?"
      Mother of two

Yes, some button gets pushed when we become grandmothers. The frustration expressed by the mother of a 9-year-old and 7-year-old, asked how she feels about her children's grandmothers, reflects the shift in power and roles once women become grandmothers.

When we were mothers, we were the role models. We didn't serve ice cream as a substitute for a meal because that is not a healthy way to live, and we were responsible for teaching our children what was healthy – for the long term. Now, our roles are different. We have passed the baton to our daughters or daughters-in-law, and, **if they are doing a good job,** we feel confident in letting up on the reins a bit.

Of course, it's easier. And, of course, it's more fun. We did the hard part. We raised you or your husbands. Now, we feel like we deserve a little rest. And, the right to break the rules you've set from time to time. Because, our influence is short-term and temporary. Your influence is long-term and permanent.

Besides, we promise to abide by your rules, mostly. Your rules are a combination of our rules, your husband's rules, his mother's rules, and what you have learned from your peers and today's experts. We only know what we did when

> *Granny-Guru's*
> **Grains of Wisdom:**
> **Parents set the rules**. Grandparents teach that rules are not the same as the law of gravity.

you or your husband were little and we were synthesizing all

Ice Cream is not a meal!

those sources. Forgive us if we think we did a pretty good job of raising you or your husband. We think you are wonderful. We understand you are doing this for the first time. So were we. We trust your instincts. But, unlike you, we have the perspective to know that expert opinion changes, or, at least, new experts come into fashion. Let us remind you that your own common sense is your best source of wisdom, but we'd be happy to share our opinions. We'll try to keep them to a minimum, knowing you will rarely ask for them. And, if we wait until asked, you'll miss some of the wisdom we could share.

When I was about ten, I remember going for a walk with my grandmother. I was eating candy, and dropped some on the ground. My Mom's rule had always been, if it falls on the ground, leave it there. You don't eat food off the ground. My grandmother picked it up, inspected it, dusted it off and handed it back to me. "It's fine," she pronounced. I thought the world had changed on its axis. I ate the candy, and was never so picky about such things again. While today, studies show us that my Mom was right, the 5-second rule does not keep germs off the food we drop, I still appreciate my grandmother's opening my eyes to a new way to be in the world.

What we are trying to do is teach that sometimes, you can break the rules and the world does not stop turning. With time, this lesson turns into the independence to know that just because someone is black, wheelchair-bound, gay, foreign, slow, or homeless does not give others the right to walk over them, whether there are laws to protect them or not. That just because it has always been done this way doesn't mean it has to be done this way. That just because everyone else is saying it cannot be done does not mean we should quit trying to see if it can. That just because no one else has climbed that mountain does not mean it cannot be climbed.

We hope we are teaching independence of thought, and, that breaking the rules with judgment can be a pretty good way to live.

And, you thought it was just a bowl of ice cream.

I'm Irrelevant (G)

"When my husband was alive, we would just drop in on our sons and grandchildren, because he had a good relationship with our sons. Now, I always call first, but only one daughter-in-law includes me in their lives. The others keep me at arm's length."
                          Four sons, eight grandchildren

When these four sons were growing up, they traveled the world with their Army dad. Army families learn to be close because they are constantly moving into new places and making new friends. And, this mother learned how to keep her family close with many shared activities. She expected to do the same as a Grandmother, and, while her husband was still alive, this was possible. Her sons and grandchildren all lived nearby. Some of her grandchildren could walk to her house after school. She organized weekly dinners at her house for the entire family. She and her husband had weekly lunches with grandchildren and their mothers. They dropped in on their sons and grandchildren frequently.

Now, that has all changed. The weekly lunches ended when it became clear they were no longer welcome. The weekly dinners have shrunk as grandchildren have aged and become involved in their own Sunday activities. This grandmother believes her daughters-in-law prefer that she call first, instead of dropping in unannounced. And, visits to a now-distant family are shortened, as in-law visits can be a strain for

> *Granny-Guru*'s **Grains of Wisdom: Your children need you even when they are adults.** Maybe not as much. They have other loyalties and priorities. And, they expect you to take care of yourself, like you always did. Maybe they haven't yet learned the power has shifted and you need them now. But, you're still their mother.

daughters-in-law, who bear primary responsibility for entertaining.

I dated an Army brat in college who had been to 13 schools in 12 years. He coped by being involved in sports. Every school had a sports program. And, school athletes could quickly integrate into school life, with a built-in set of friends on their team. But, he also made himself a personal rule. No more than three dates with the same girl. Anticipating a forced break-up, he never allowed himself to get close enough to anyone to deal with the loss he knew was coming. We met for Cokes after a shared class for an entire semester. We only ever had two dates, preserving the possibility of a third, because it would be our last. Though he had been looking forward to being in one place for four years, in the end, he did not know how to do it. He left school and enrolled in the Army after one year of college.

The boys in this family may have made their own rules about how to be in this world, what it meant to settle down in one place. For the years their father was around, they might have relished the closeness of family, all in one place, finally. But, their wives likely came from different backgrounds. Not feeling the pent-up need for family closeness, they likely viewed it as too close. Stifling, even, as they struggled to establish their own families, with their own rules, mutually agreed on with their husbands, as new family units, not negotiated with in-laws. With children aging into their own busy schedules and a newly-widowed mother-in-law lacking the anchor of a long-term marriage, the rules suddenly changed. The closeness she had treasured, they may have now felt free to discard, at a time when she may have needed it most.

This is clearly a time to renegotiate agreements about acceptable, even welcomed levels of time together. The grandchildren are growing fast. This grandmother wants to be tied into their lives while they still value her presence. But, her sons still need her too. Is it possible to have some time alone, lunches or dinners, with her sons, taking this responsibility off the shoulders of the busy daughters-in-law, who have their own families to be responsible for, after all, and giving it back to the sons who need it? Is it possible to establish routines of phone calls, webcam visits, email or text updates with grandchildren independent of their mothers? *The New York Times* interviewed families using webcams between grandchildren and their grandparents, highlighted in a November 26, 2008 article, "Grandma's on the Computer Screen" discussing just this option for distant grandparents.

This grandmother has much to share and, as she knows only too well, only a brief window to share it in.

Your Grandchild is More Important than Tennis (M)

"My mother would drop anything to be with her grandchild. But, my mother-in-law is busy with tennis and her dogs. We have to book her two months in advance to get on her schedule."
  Mother who recently lost her mother

"Baby-sitting is limited to two hours. It is hard to go out to dinner in a two-hour window. Despite an open-door policy, there are no drop-in visits. Obviously missed opportunities when in the neighborhood of a nearby grandchild. No phone calls to talk to the grandchild. No surprise trips to local activities, just Grandmother and grandchild."

The only surviving grandparent, still young, busy with her own job and activities, re-married, bears a heavy burden in this family. The expectation that she will supplant the other missed Grandmother, and, perhaps, the longed-for contact with a too-early gone Mother. Perhaps, different expectations about frequency of contact. Perhaps, simply personality differences.

To be fair, she does respond when asked. She baby-sits. She joins the family for outings. She comes over. But, it is all initiated by the young family, not by the Grandmother. And, she never asks to keep the grandchild overnight, usually a great privilege for grandparents who

Granny-Guru's **Grains of Wisdom: At first, negotiating frequency of visits is difficult and delicate**. Expectations vary so widely. But, eventually, we all have to have that discussion, and, maybe, keep having it, as circumstances change. No guilt. Just love.

then get to spoil their grandchildren rotten before handing them back to their parents.

She must not understand the longing she is missing, for her to be that Grandmother who drops everything for the hug of a grandchild. Perhaps she still has not learned the lesson that life is too short to waste. Children grow up, lose interest in the close connections families try to preserve, then want them again when their own children bring them back. She must not be in the same cycle this family is. And, they don't want her to ignore the fact that the cycle relentlessly moves on.

This Grandmother has moved on in her life. A new husband, after having lost the father of her son. Her own new family to nourish. She clearly delights in her grandchild, but does not make the grandchild the center of her life. As is her privilege.

Still, I remember the shock of hearing that my father had been in town on business and had not bothered to call. Realizing his rudeness when he unexpectedly let this fact slip a few months later, he tried to explain with, "Well, I was busy. I knew I wasn't going to have time to see you, so I didn't call."

Remembering this some years later, I called my son between flights when I changed planes in his city. "I know you can't come out to the airport to have dinner because I won't be down long enough, but, just wanted to call." " So, Mom, what are you doing about the tornado that's about to touch down?" Waiting in the airport all night until planes started flying again in the morning, watching the reporters interview all the stranded passengers. That's what. And, we still didn't get to see each other.

The Money They Spend! (G)

"When we were first married, we were very careful about the money we spent. We understood that bigger expenses were down the road, so we lived modestly and saved."
Grandmother of three

When I was first married, my husband came home one day, exasperated by a young secretary in his office. My husband was a newly-minted Army officer, supporting a wife and son in our first two-bedroom apartment. The secretary was single, living at home, paying no room and board, making more than he did, and constantly complaining about not having enough money to live on. It was highly annoying. What were her parents trying to teach her?

I have my own stories of paying $25 for a used crib from yard sales, twice. Eating bag lunches at work. Throwing out a budget because we could not live on the estimated expenses, and, then, just not buying clothes for three years. Not buying toys for our children for the

> *Granny-Guru*'s **Grains of Wisdom: Savings are not for tomorrow. They are for five, ten and twenty years from now.** If you're lucky, you won't need them until then.

first several years of their lives, except at Christmas and birthdays, preferring to let them play with old milk cartons to pour water in and out of, Hershey's cocoa cans with beans or dried rice to shake, oatmeal boxes for drums, handmade teddy bears and stuffed lions, and homemade sweaters, mittens and hats. And, I didn't even grow up in the Depression. But, I did grow up with Depression-era parents. Every time I asked my mother for money for something, she took out a small basket she used to keep the change left over from the allowance she and Dad allotted for weekly groceries and told me what it was going to be used for, usually shoes. I never got the money. But, I got the message. The allowances we were given in elementary school ended by the age of 12 as we all figured out ways to make our own spending money.

So, I understood that money was not unlimited. This translated into a similar understanding that while there are an endless supply of cute baby things you can buy, the bigger expenses come later – school, glasses, braces, college, to say nothing of a house. Some of whatever you are making today had better be put aside for those larger expenses in your future.

What I did not understand that this grandmother is speaking to is that it is easy for my generation and this generation to rely on two full-time incomes in the early years of a marriage, when raises may come frequently. It may be less understood by a generation used to having substantial spending money that a large portion of those two incomes needs to be committed to tomorrow's bigger expenses, including the freedom to stop one of those incomes if someone is sick, between jobs, pregnant, staying at home with children, going to school, or starting their own company.

My banker told me recently that when he was between jobs for three months, a neighbor watched him mowing his lawn, seemingly quite relaxed and told him, "If either my wife or I lost our job, we would be facing bankruptcy within two paychecks." My banker and I had the same reaction to this statement. How do they sleep at night?!

This generation, cushioned by good jobs right out of college, needs to devote ten to fifty percent of a second income to savings, at least until there is enough money in the bank that six months out-of-work is not a catastrophe. This may seem like a lot until you think about the hardship it would cause if the family income were cut by fifty percent if one of them lost a job unexpectedly. It's a lot harder to cut expenses when income is cut suddenly than to plan to live on less. There are easy ways to do it. Have ten percent taken out of your paycheck before you even see it and sent directly to a savings account. Have half of every raise sent to that same savings account; half of every bonus.

A family should be contributing to savings accounts for a house, college for each child, and a buffer for big-ticket items, like going back to school. And, if they're smart, they will take a lesson from the *Rich Dad, Poor Dad*[26] philosophy. Set aside money that is only used to make money, independent of a paycheck. This could start with savings bonds and certificates of deposit, and eventually grow into investments in real estate or the stock market, or starting a business.

Then, they can buy the cute baby things.

P.S. To get children started on good financial principles, check out Mrs. Money, a former banker who now devotes herself to teaching elementary-school children about good money management. You'll love her four-part piggy bank, designed to show children they need to put money aside for spending, saving, donating and investing.[27]

Check out our blog post on financial literacy and the four-slot piggy bank. http://newgrandmas.com/financialliteracy

---

[26] Get the book, *Rich Dad, Poor Dad: What the Rich Teach Their Kids About Money That the Poor and Middle Class Do Not!* Here: http://newgrandmas.com/richdadpoordad

[27] Money Savvy Generation: Fiscal Fitness for Kids™ http://www.msgen.com/assembled/fiscal_fitness.html

I Would Like to Say Things Sometimes (G)

"Don't you think it would be a good idea for the grandchildren to play outside more? Don't you think they are eating too many sweets? If you don't stick with 'No' now, it's going to be a lot harder to stick with it later."
Grandmother of eight, three daughters

"But, of course, I don't say anything. Unless they are handling the good china, you can't really say anything because it would be seen as criticism. And, I try to stay positive with my grandchildren, so I don't say anything to them either that would be different from what their parents allow. But, sometimes, I just wish I could say something that would be helpful as they raise their children."

When did exercise, good food habits and consistent discipline come to be seen as fuddy-duddy values? Or is it simply that the emotional baggage between a mother and daughter is too strong a filter to hear any useful advice?

My mother was an expert at manipulating us into doing what she wanted. You may wear the red sweater or the green sweater today. How about the blue one? Or a jacket instead? Or no sweater? It's a neat trick offering a child choices

> **Granny-Guru's Grains of Wisdom: Grandmas sometimes have advice of value.** Ask them to tell you what they aren't saying. It should start with, "You're a wonderful Mother."

among which you don't care what the answer is, trying to divert them from choosing what you would object to. And, it works for toddlers, just learning they have the power to make choices. Somehow, though, she was able to age-adjust the manipulation, and hide it.

Although I didn't really understand it had been happening until I got married, at some level, I resented it. And, resisted any interference, or even suggestions, until my children were grown. Perhaps this is a natural step in independence. Mother, please. I'd rather do it myself. So goes the old commercial. A hit because its message so closely mirrors what we'd like to say when Mom is offering helpful suggestions.

Yet, my mother did provide suggestions. She had been the role model when I was in fifth grade, handling the next-door neighbor's newborn and teaching me to put a hand under its floppy head, supporting its neck, and explaining why. She and I both regretted the fact that a close friend of hers moved away just after her baby was born as we'd both expected to be a large part of that child's life. But, I did see my Mom gently, unperturbed, whisper and coo to that crying baby. I learned that just because babies cry, you don't have to get upset with them. In fact, it's better if you don't. Calm Mom. Eventually, calm baby.

But, by the time I had my own children, I assumed that Mom had done her job, teaching me to have my own judgment. I was no longer looking to her for advice or suggestions or role modeling. And, there was that emotional baggage. Don't you think you've raised me right? Don't you think I can handle it on my own now?

She was able to break through this wall from time to time. She showed me, by doing it herself, that a toddler can play ball, after a fashion. That is, you don't wait until a toddler can play ball to start the game. You set them up on the floor, with their legs spread wide, so you can roll a ball between their legs and start to teach them the give and take of playing with a ball. Eventually, they get it. I guess, until she did that, I thought a child would have to be a lot older before you could play ball with them. She taught me you can be pro-active in teaching them things they are too young to do on their own.

But, the implication with suggestions is that the parents don't have any judgment of their own. So, Grandmas try not to give them. But, what if there really is something they could help with? What if there is something they are noticing that you could course-correct, if you just had some outside, objective feedback?

This is the question Moms need to ask themselves. Am I missing something? After all, Grandmas don't just have opinions and experience; they have an outsider's perspective. And, that's the problem. They don't see themselves as outsiders, after all. They see themselves as insiders. You are their children. How could they not be insiders with your children when they know just how you acted at the same age?

For that matter, parents usually listen to stories of what they were like at that age. Because it does give them insight. But, grandparents really are outsiders when it comes to what you might be doing differently. Give them a chance to let you know what they've noticed. You'll both be glad. They promise to do it with love. After all, they think most of what you do with their precious grandchildren is spot on.

If Grandmas list more than three things they think Moms should be doing different, you have permission to end the conversation. End it with, "Thank you. You've given me something to think about." Then, do what you think is right. Grandmas, stop when you see that you've exceeded your advice ration. And, remind them what a good job you think they're doing. You can never hear that too often.

The Mouth On That Child! (G)

"I got in trouble with both the Mom and the Dad when I spanked my grandchild with a spatula for bad language. Elementary school age is old enough to show respect. I just couldn't stand to listen to that mouth anymore."
Grandmother of two

Respect and discipline. At what point are Grandmas allowed to blow up over what they see as an obvious lack of discipline and the need to teach children to respect their elders? This grandmother recognized that she was crossing boundaries in stepping in where her own child had apparently not demanded the respect most adults require of a child. But, in her own home, she eventually decided her precious grandchild had crossed a wildly inappropriate boundary.

At a recent Karaoke outing, one of the twenty-somethings apologized to Granny-Guru in advance of a song he sang, then came over afterwards to see if I had survived the shock of the language he used. "It's not that I haven't heard that language before," I told him. "It's that I've never heard anyone sing using that language." So, the boundaries of good taste have changed. That's not new. Every generation pushes the boundaries of good taste. What seems new to boomer Grandmas, though, is the age and settings in which children are allowed to use bad language, without consequences from their parents.

From a Grandma's perspective, the issue is not whether parents think it is ok, or funny, or not worth the time or a battle, but, whether they are thinking down the road to such behavior in other situations that would normally demand respect. Foul language with a teacher, a policeman, a judge, in church, even in a business negotiation will limit that grandchild's opportunities in uncountable ways. The world will not be so gentle in explaining the facts of life. Don't grandparents rate that kind of respect?

Is there room for foul language? To express explosive anger? Yes. But, this is a weapon you use for emphasis, not something a child plays with routinely. A choice a woman may make to put men at ease, as a young woman journalist, recently returned from being embedded with Army troops during the war in Iraq said she did. Her anticipatory swearing allowed her companions and protectors to laugh and set aside their respectful behavior in favor of the quick responses they would need for life-threatening situations. It is not an elementary school habit.

> *Granny-Guru*'s **Grains of Wisdom: Respect may have to be earned as adults, but it should be demanded of children.**

Children are used to acting and speaking differently among their friends than they do around adults. The question is, why aren't parents demanding the respect of their children that appropriate language conveys? Perhaps one frustrated Grandma can be forgiven for reaching her limit with her precious grandchild, hoping to save that child from much more severe consequences in the wider world. And this Grandma felt forgiven when she was recently told by another adult in her grandchild's life that Grandma was one of her favorite people.

Parents have not only the right, but the responsibility for ensuring that children understand what respectful behavior looks like and when it is important. Grandparents should not have to teach this lesson, but can be forgiven for expecting it.

They Are So Ungrateful (G)

"I send my grandchildren gifts, but, not only do they not write and thank me, when they come and see me they don't even thank me. Doesn't their Mom teach them any manners?"
Grandmother

Mom is busy. And, she is deciding which of the hundreds of things she wants her children to do that are important enough to ride herd on them to make sure they get done. Piano practice? Soccer meets? Homework? Tooth brushing? Chores? Making sure they get off to school every day, with food or money for lunch. Clean clothes. Recent baths. Signed permission slips for school trips. Signed report cards. Signed vaccination records. Shoes that fit. Pants that are long enough. Book bags that are packed and unpacked every day. Treats for school events, Cub Scout meetings, recitals. And, Mom probably has a job of her own to think about.

And, if letters are too much to ask, how about a phone call? How about remembering to say thank you in person? Sure, Mom should remember to prompt her children to say thank you the next time they see you, but life has gone on a hundred different side trips since then. Just ask. "How did you like …?" Without a penalty for not thinking to bring it up themselves.

Though thank-you letters eventually dropped off in my family, our distant grandparents' request was not just to thank them, but at least to let them know we got the gifts. What did we ungrateful children do? Eventually, we left it to our parents to communicate that, indeed, we had received the gifts and liked them a lot. And, eventually, the grandparents did what they had threatened to do. They stopped sending them. But, that just meant we no longer had the regular reminders of our grandparents' love and attention. We knew they loved us. Gifts or no gifts did not change that. We just weren't reminded anymore.

So, what is the answer? Grandparents see a thank you letter not just as an acknowledgement of the care and thought that went into selecting, buying, wrapping and sending a gift. But, as a matter of respect to their position as grandparent

> ***Granny-Guru's* Grains of Wisdom: Silence does not mean disrespect.** Insert yourself back in the loop by writing to your grandchildren.

and their role in watching over and delighting in the growth of their grandchildren. And, as a sign that children are being raised to understand the formal rules of society. To show gratitude to adults they respect. Every Human Resources guide to interviewees says, "Send a follow-up note after the interview. You will distinguish yourself from the pack because so few people do it."

Former President George H. W. Bush, a famously prolific letter writer, is author of the book, *All the Best, George Bush: My Life in Letters and Other Writings*.[28] I was once sent a hand-written postcard by a CEO responding to a letter I had sent him. He made a habit of responding personally to selected letters when he was traveling. This personal touch astounded and impressed me. How do we give our children that gift, the ability to astound, impress, stand out from the crowd? We are trying to do it by expecting thank-you letters, but that isn't working. And, this is the most tightly connected generation ever. Do we have to get Twitter or learn to send text messages? Probably not that. But, we do not have to take it personally. We do not have to see it as a sign of disrespect or poor parenting, but rather as a sign of busy times.

It may be sloppy. You may wish children were learning the formal rules of our grandparents. But, busier lives means something will be dropped. Letter writing is crowded out by

---

[28] Get the book, *All the Best*, here: http://newgrandmas.com/allthebest

keeping up with the latest computer technology, a loop grandparents may not be part of.

Probably the best answer is modeling. I still treasure the letters my father sent me when I was in college. Each one took a theme about life as I was learning it and gave me guidelines. My favorite was how, how much and who to tip. I didn't answer them, but, forty years later, I still remember them fondly.

Grandparents could do worse than writing their grandchildren. And, who knows? They might be moved to answer. The post office works both ways.

Besides, you don't have to wait for a phone call. A well-timed call just after the package has arrived, or been opened before a party, may get just the "Thank you" you were hoping for.

Chapter 4
High School and Beyond

I've Never Been Shy (G)

"I've never been shy about giving my opinions. But, I find myself giving less and less advice, because I've noticed the total package of how my grandchildren are being raised is working well."
   Grandmother of sixteen, Ph.D. in childhood development

It's the details, isn't it? Our opinions about how often a baby should be fed, whether on-demand or on-schedule, pacifiers or no, breast-feeding or no, cloth diapers or disposable have been formed by hard-won experience. But now, these details need to fit with the personality, child-raising experience and judgment of the mothers of our precious grandchildren. Their experiences and their understanding of the world today, its demands on their lives and how expert opinions have changed in the last forty years is theirs to inform their decisions, not ours.

At first, some grandmothers bite their tongues rather than step on the tender feelings of a new mother, so as to give her a chance to establish her own rules, find her own pace, trust her own judgment. But, some grandmothers feel they would be cheating the new mother if they held back advice earned through an entire generation of child rearing.

This isn't about how mothers deal with this welcome or unwelcome advice, but, rather, how grandmothers learn to be in their new role of advice-giver, instead of being responsible for a new life. It is learned in a thousand decisions made by new mothers and reviewed by grandmothers. From day care arrangements to school choices, from indoor and outdoor play

> *Granny-Guru*'s **Grains of Wisdom: Letting go of the advice-giving role may be a gradual process, earned like the first set of keys to the family car by learning trust in the new mother's judgment.**

options to seeking or following a doctor's advice, mothers and grandmothers learn a new way to negotiate, because it is no longer about what a now-grown child is doing, but, their influence on a young child. And, the grandmother's influence is no longer direct. It is once removed, accessible to a grandchild only through the permission and actions of the child's mother.

My own mother left me to my own devices in childrearing. She believed she had raised me to have good judgment and that would show in my decisions. While I welcomed the hands-off freedom, I would have welcomed more stories about how she raised us and why she made the decisions she did. We all had our own stories about the privilege of being served orange juice in bed when we were seniors in high school, a rather gentler wake-up call than the usual alarm clock. Serving each other meals when the first one came down with measles so we would all get it over with before school started. But, children remember different stories than their parents. And, they can only make up the reasoning behind adult decisions.

Opinions, stories, books – all help shape the actions and beliefs of those we share them with. Peer opinions are most often believed, but stories from across the generations can be the most valuable.

Give Your Child Some Relationship with God (G)

"God needs to be part of your child's life. It gives them something to fight against later. But, at least, they know where to start, even if they decide to reject religion as adults."
  Mother of three, Grandmother of three

"After a dear friend died, her daughter told me, 'I want to pray. But, I don't even know where to start. I've never been churched.' So, I would tell my children, at least give your children a chance to experience a relationship with God. Even if they decide to reject the religion given to them as children, they have something on which to make that decision."

This grandmother's faith is heavily committed to service and she has lived that value with a weekly gift of her professional services. But, she sees her faith as the anchor that gives that service meaning, and wishes it for her grandchildren.

When I was a teenager, one of my best baby-sitting clients once told me, "Whatever you do, make sure you marry a Christian." She even went on to say that she was not really a committed Christian when she got married, but felt lucky that when she decided to commit, her husband already had. As I did not share her faith, I took her

> *Granny-Guru*'s **Grains of Wisdom: Religious upbringing. What is a parent's responsibility?** To give children the tools they need to see them through life's vagaries. If spiritual, if family, if neighborhood or culture. What is larger than our own personal lives and interests? What ties us to the larger family of the world? What sustains us when life is not fair?

advice in the larger sense that I should marry someone whose values I shared.

I took these values to be respect, commitment to family, and honesty. Service to others was not a large part of my value system. But, an open exploration of a spiritual path was. And, when I changed my faith as a teenager, it was largely because this open discussion was shut down at the time I started asking questions. But, having been raised in one faith, explored several others and settled on one I was more comfortable with, I, too, like this grandmother, believed that at least I'd had the option to choose from experience. Now that I think of it, my parents stopped taking us to church when I was five and I'd picked a church one of my friends in the neighborhood went to because they had a choir.

As an adult, I came to believe that the values you model are the real foundation on which your children will rely. Still, I noticed when my son and I volunteered at a food bank run by the Salvation Army, and later helped out at Habitat for Humanity, while many of the other volunteers were from corporate groups or Scout troops, most were from church groups.

Religion is probably less open to discussion, even within families, than politics, less even, than sex. It is personal, emotional and intimate. Depending on it, as many do, to see us through the difficult circumstances of life, the death of a parent or child, grievous unexplained, too early loss, we cannot open up our raw emotions to someone else's suggestions about how we should conduct our own spiritual journey. Religion gives comfort, provides community, is an outlet for our compassion and instinct to serve.

Your actions show your children what values you believe important. But, they will choose their own path. Is the assurance of faith, its rituals, its steadiness when life's circumstances change a reason to make sure your children and grandchildren have this opportunity to grow up with a foundation that goes beyond values?

Well, after 9/11, I played the hymns of my childhood. I still take comfort in them. But, I would not return to that faith. Your children will learn your values. They watch you. What rituals are you sharing with your children? What will comfort them? How will they serve and connect themselves to the wider world?

Tell Them You Love Them (G)

"I would tell mothers three things about raising children. Tell them you love them. Give them rules to follow and make sure they follow them. Take them to church."
 3 children, 11 grandchildren, 22 great-grandchildren, 3 great-great grandchildren

Easy to say. Hard to do. It's like telling someone in the stock market to buy low and sell high. Well, yeah. But, timing is everything. So, when you're in the middle of raising children, working, paying bills, making sure everyone gets three meals a day and clothes that fit and are clean, a household that runs and is clean enough for company from time to time, and, a life (!), do you remember to take time out to tell your children you love them?

Stroke their hair, pat their shoulder at quiet moments and tell them how important they are to you, how glad you are to have them in your life. This great-great grandmother admits that she didn't tell her children she loved them when they were growing up. She thought they knew by her actions. But, when one of them finally asked, "Why don't you ever say you love me?" she realized it was time to start. Actions are what counts, but, we all like to hear we are loved.

That one is hard for me, too, because my parents never did. They had the notion that it was enough to be there when we needed them, and that we would just know they loved us by that steadfastness, without its ever being said. The closest either came was a few months before my father died. He was telling me about a television show he had watched where a parent told a child they loved them. He looked at me, nearly tearing up, "I could just never do that." And, he never did, but, I got the message. My mother finally told me in a letter that I kept in the dining room for ten years. She never told me in person, though she lived with us for two years at the end of her life. I didn't even learn to hug until I married into a family of huggers.

Rules are easy. Enforcement is hard. Because children are always testing the limits. No matter what promise you make about consequences, they turn right around and do the forbidden thing, just to see if you mean it. And, if you don't, they will keep testing until they find out where the limits really are. And testing. And testing.

> ***Granny-Guru*'s Grains of Wisdom: Grandparents have perspective.** Grandparents understand there are some fundamental rules to live by that are not affected by fashion, new discoveries or experts. Some things have not changed in the forty years since we started raising our own children.

While Grandma's rules may be different than Mom's, children have no trouble keeping them straight. My grandson always goes directly to the closet where his toys are kept whenever he comes to visit. He knows where the stepstool is kept and which counter he can safely push it up to. Fortunately, my house doesn't change much, largely because I no longer have an active family of children who forget to put things back where they belong. But, this reliability, this predictability, this stability is precisely what builds trust, an extension of safety into the world that Grandma can provide simply by keeping the toys in the same place.

Church, synagogue, a community, extended family. In our neighborhood, when our children were growing up, no child was allowed to cross a busy street by themselves to get to the 7/11 until they were 12 years old. A rite of passage that everyone agreed on.

Values that adults agree on and talk about that are consistent with their actions. Contributing to and participating in a larger community than your own family. Taking your children or grandchildren to church or neighborhood or family gatherings and hearing adults talk about values helps a child set their own, giving them a bond across and among generations that simply cannot be provided by parents alone. This is that village so many people talk about, helping you raise your children.

They Really Grow Up Fast (G)

"I pretty much say anything I feel like saying, but one thing I would like to caution is that they really grow up fast."
3 children, 5 grandchildren

"You don't realize. Everything seems like it will be this way forever, and before you know it, they are grown up. Spend time with them every day. Listen to them. Enjoy them."

When you're in the middle of raising children, you don't have the perspective this grandmother has. It is only when you can look back that you can see how short that child-raising period is.

I remember standing in a grocery-store line when an older woman admired my beautiful son. She said, "I just want to take him home with me." I assured her there were many 2 AMs when I would be grateful for her to come take him home. It was a joke, of course. But, I wanted to remind her that he wasn't always as cute and easy as he was at that moment.

But, she was trying to tell me what this grandmother knows. Sure, there are times when children are cranky, willful, troublesome. But, these are far outweighed by the delightfulness of their presence in our lives. And, those years when they are completely dependent on us do not last. They are both a burden and a joy. A burden because of the responsibility of making sure their lives turn out the best they can possibly be, while we are, at the same

> **Granny-Guru's Grains of Wisdom: Diaper changing, school routines, friends and activities are all intense at the time.** But, child rearing is a 25-year window. Although it comes at a time in your life when everything else is happening too, it is not the whole of a 60-to-80-year life.

They really grow up fast.

time, making a living, figuring out our own jobs and marriages. And, a joy because you simply cannot imagine a life without them once they have touched yours.

And, once they are no longer dependent, you realize how full your lives were when they were in them. When they have finished school, started jobs, moved into their own places, started making their own decisions about their lives, which may or may not agree with yours – teenagehood was really your last shot at enforcing your opinions – you realize how short it was, after all.

You then may have influence, but not the final word. They may live close or far away, but are no longer turning to you for advice on their daily lives. You may see them often or infrequently, but they are making their own way in the world and need time to focus on that task.

And, you suddenly realize. Wow. That was fast.

I tell people that my age, the ages of my children and the length of my marriage are imaginary numbers. Because time is not linear. It bends according to the way we use it. This grandmother's insight speaks to that truth.

Use the precious time you have with your children as though it could end tomorrow.

Because, one day it will.

About the Author

The author became a grandmother in 2005. She did not know before then that two very different grandchildren could both be perfect. She should have known. She already had two perfect children.

But, she had opinions that she did not feel she could share with the new parents. After all, they were just learning how to be parents.

And, she had finished her job of raising children. It was time to let go to the next generation, whom she both admired and trusted.

So, she decided to ask other grandmothers, and, eventually, mothers, if they had opinions that they had been reluctant to share. Or, that they had shared yet still felt strongly about.

Of course, they did!

Granny-Guru started asking for these opinions, and you've just read the results.

We hope you enjoyed these articles and we look forward to seeing you again when upcoming books are available.

Coming soon:

- *Fun with Grandchildren: 10-Minute Science*
- *New Grandmas: Raising Children Has Changed*

Contact us: Send us an email if you want to know when our new books are available. We will add you to our email list for news.

Follow us on Facebook, Twitter, LinkedIn or Pinterest by searching for Carol Covin.

Subscribe to our RSS feed: http://newgrandmas.com/rss

With much love to you and yours,

Granny-Guru
Bristow, Virginia
Web site: http://newgrandmas.com
email: mail@newgrandmas.com

Index

Acid reflux	57
ADHD	85
Advice	
From grandmother	21, 28, 50, 98, 107
From mother-in-law	19, 29, 43
From peers	21
Allergies	57
Baby blankets	50
Baby-sitting	23, 63, 93
Bad language	73, 101
Bragging	76
Bread made in bed	65
Breast feeding	19
Burns	51
Caffeine	57
Car seats	31
Changes	26, 35
Communication	
With children	83 112
With grandchildren	38, 75
With in-laws	26, 43
Community	109, 112
Crying baby	24, 26, 47, 99
Dating	66
Deaf	14
Diaper rash	51
Discipline	45, 47, 73, 98, 101, 112
Disability	85
Distant grandparenting	16, 19, 26, 38, 52, 73, 103
Drop-in (see Visits, Unannounced)	
Entertainment	63
Exercise	98
Fairness	38, 71
Fathers	
Age appropriate	36
Army family	44, 90
Away from home	26, 29, 103
Love	61, 71, 112
Mother/son visits	90, 93
Food	39, 43, 57, 77, 87, 98
Grandma's Rules	38, 45, 47, 73, 87, 112
Grandpa	63
Helicopter parents	83
Hyperactive	85

Letters	16, 25, 103
Love	112
Manners	103
Money	95
Names	12
Newborns	19, 21, 50, 99
Nursing	19
Pacifiers	50
Pooping	21
Presents	
Money	40
Number	40
Thank-you	103
Religion	109, 112
Respect	14, 19, 23, 31, 43, 45, 50, 73, 101, 103, 109
Safety	31, 35, 47, 54, 112
SIDS	50
Singing	14
Smoking	32
Spanking	101
Spoiling	52, 93
Stories	30, 50, 52, 98, 107
Sugar	57, 77, 80
Television	63
Throwing balls	63, 98
Time	16, 19, 23, 26, 38, 40, 63, 80, 90, 115
Trust	107, 112
Visits	
From a distance	19, 26, 40, 52, 57, 73, 80, 90
Unannounced	93

Sign up today for our email list and get a free copy of "How to Leap the Generation Gap: 58 Reasons Child-Rearing Is Different Today. Sign up at http://newgrandmas.com Below is a sample.

In my day...
Today...

Babies and Newborns	
1. In my day... Babies sleep on stomachs Today... Babies sleep on backs	SIDS (Sudden Infant Death Syndrome), also called crib death, has been reduced from 5,000 a year to fewer than 3,000 a year with the campaign to inform everyone about putting babies down to sleep on their backs at night and for naps, begun in 1992. This is balanced by "tummy time" when babies are awake and on their tummy to build the muscles in their necks as they raise their heads. http://www.nichd.nih.gov/publications/pubs/safe_sleep_gen.cfm
2. In my day... Baby blankets Today Baby sleepers	Additional risk factors for SIDS include overheating and obstruction of airflow. Current recommendations include taking out all loose blankets from a crib. A recent study showed that putting a fan in a baby's room reduced the incidence of SIDS by 72%. http://children.webmd.com/news/20081006/sleeping-with-fan-may-lower-sids-risk http://parenting.ivillage.com/bab

	y/bsafety/0,,871g09t7-3,00.html
3. In my day… Seat belts Today… Car seats	Car seat laws vary by state and age of child, but generally include a backward-facing car seat up to one year, and forward facing, preferably in the back seat to avoid air bags, up to 40 pounds. http://www.elitecarseats.com/custserv/custserv.jsp?pageName=car_seat_laws
11. In my day… Guess why baby is crying Today… Baby sign language	Thought to increase a child's language ability and decrease their and parents' frustration over asking for simple things, like milk, teaching babies sign language before they can talk is a common practice now. http://www.babies-and-sign-language.com/

Sign up for our email list today and get your free copy of the entire report. http://newgrandmas.com

Get our daily posts from Newgrandmas.com in your email!

http://newgrandmas.com/blogbyemail

www.ingramcontent.com/pod-product-compliance
Lightning Source LLC
Chambersburg PA
CBHW071519040426
42444CB00008B/1716